Bill Robert
Psalm 27:1

From
Make-Believe
to
Reality

KENNETH DODSON

From Make-Believe to Reality

The Bill Roberts Story

Fleming H. Revell Company
Old Tappan, New Jersey

Scripture quotations in this volume are from the King James Version of the Bible.

Library of Congress Cataloging in Publication Data

Dodson, Kenneth.
    From make-believe to reality.

    1. Roberts, Bill.   2.   Conversion.
I.   Title.
BV4935.R57D62   248'.24 ₍B₎   73–8802
ISBN 0–8007–0614–5

TO
Barbara Roberts,
one of the Lord's modest jewels

From
Make-Believe
to
Reality

1

Billy Roberts became an actor at the age of six and he played to the largest and most attentive crowd he could find. There were handicaps, for he lived in a small town. In fact, the biggest thing about the town was its name, Waxahachie, Texas, and the largest and most attentive crowd Billy could play before was a captive audience in his grandmother's chicken house.

There were advantages in this for Billy. His audience never seemed bored by his little plays and stories. They weren't like the grown folks with their impatient, "Oh, another time, Billy. That's enough for now; run out and play." On these hot, still Texas afternoons it was quiet in the chicken house. The hens went about their business of laying eggs or scratching for food in a respectful sort of way. The aging rooster stood still with his feathers drooping, head cocked to a side, and gave more attention to Billy than to his hens. So, in a modest chicken house in Waxahachie, Bill Roberts, his mind's eye already gazing into the future toward a tremendously successful career upon the finest of Broadway's stages, worked hard upon his childish repertoire.

Billy's grandmother, Lena, was one of a family of several girls and no sons. Private tutors and music teachers came to the house. A governess taught them the graces and decorum expected of a lady. Lena knew next to nothing about life beyond her father's aristocratic home. James Peavler, a young man working on the plantation, fell in love with Lena and at fifteen years of age she eloped with him. Immediately her father disowned her.

As he grew up, little Billy Roberts had a warm and close relationship with his grandmother. He loved her and he loved the dreamworld which she represented for him.

Billy's grandparents had moved from Tennessee to Texas. Grandfather was a man of the earth, loved farming, raising animals—a plainspoken, hardworking man. Grandmother's part was bearing eleven children without any help, toiling manually over a scrubboard in a number 2½ tub, making her own lye soap in the backyard, making and mending clothes for the surviving ten of her children. That was the life expected of a woman, but she never complained.

As many a girl before her in a similar situation, Billy's mother escaped by marriage and immediately found herself in a more difficult situation than before. At nineteen she married Chapman Thomas Roberts, a man fifteen years her senior. His first wife had died during the terrible influenza epidemic following World War One, which killed thousands of people. There were no wonder drugs in those days. The flu victim often developed pneumonia. After that, it was a question of having the stamina to survive the climax of the illness. She was one who did not. The widowed Chapman Roberts was left with two children, a son, Newland Roberts, and a girl, Irene.

Chapman had a quick and tremendously hot temper; he gambled and had something of a drinking problem. Not a religious man in any sense of the word, the only time he spoke the names of God or Jesus Christ was when angry.

Chapman and Willie Mae had been married six years when young Billy Roberts was born to them. Willie Mae was about twenty-five. The stepchildren, Newland and Irene, were fourteen and twelve and seemed more like a younger brother and sister to her than her children. They did not get along at all well with her. Rebellion and angry arguments greeted her efforts at discipline and their father failed to back her up. Friction was the normal atmosphere in the house. The arrival of baby Billy was no threat at all to them; he was somebody they could all love and spoil. Chapman became a doting father, lavishing loving pride and attention. At the age of two, Billy was a confident and apparently extroverted child, who thrived upon his well-received little entertainments. His sister, Irene, was his constant companion and had a deep influence on his first four or five years.

Deep trouble came after they moved to a home in Bakersfield, California. When Billy was four, his father developed a malignant brain tumor which was inoperable. Chapman still retained the appearance and drive of a young man, and his terminal illness was not only a shock to Willie Mae and the family; they seemed to be facing an impossible disaster, yet knowing all the time that it was really true.

Chapman lasted twenty-two months. During this time, Willie Mae became pregnant again—this while Chapman went through the many stages of his downhill illness. He became blind, then went through periods of being totally irrational. They would hospitalize him; he would seem to rally a bit and beg to come home. Willie Mae would bring him home, then find that she could not possibly take care of him.

One evening, ill herself and sitting on the front porch, Willie Mae heard singing from a nearby tent meeting. In spite of her illness, she dressed and went to the meeting. Regardless of the faith of her parents, she was not a Christian. Deeply moved at this tent meeting, she gave her heart to the Lord. Thus while her Billy was very young, she asked Christ into her heart. She was a very verbal person and at once began to spread the Good News.

The love between Chapman and Willie Mae grew deeper during these tragic days. She longed for him to accept the Lord and find peace. About the time that Chapman had come to the end of himself, two men came to visit him a number of times. They talked to him about Jesus Christ. Tenderly, lovingly, they urged this man, once so ill-tempered and profane, to accept the Saviour who loved him so much. He asked them about faith, about all the things in his life that had been wrong. They explained God's plan for our forgiveness and how—even in his blindness and helplessness and pain—a simple faith, like a grain of mustard seed, would be more than enough. God would keep His promise and His love never failed.

Chapman committed his life to Christ and was truly

born into the family of God. All his life he had been a forthright man. Now he asked to be baptized.

As a little boy, Billy was influenced by what was happening. Small as he was, he was aware of something new: a sense of tenderness in the home. At times he saw his father staggering in a brave effort to get about unaided. He knew that his father was very ill and everybody said now that he couldn't get well. It seemed that illness was all about him. Yet death was not something he understood, though he heard folks talking and whispering about it all the time. He loved his daddy and would crawl on the bed and have visits with him.

The last night of Chapman's life, Willie Mae was utterly worn out from keeping her bedside vigil. She was urged to go lie down on a bed in another room and they sent Billy to stay with her. His mother didn't go to sleep, but lay quiet in the darkness of the room. After a bit, Billy slid down from the bed and went quietly into the room where his father lay dying. Nobody stopped him or said anything. Billy climbed up on the old iron bed and looked down on his dying father. It was an experience that touched him deeply so that he never forgot.

On the wall was a copy of a famous painting of Christ in the Garden of Gethsemane. In the last moments of his life, Billy saw his father turn his sightless eyes in the direction in which he knew that picture to be. Across his face came a beautiful smile as if he could already see beyond sickness and pain and catch a glimpse of his Saviour's face.

Willie Mae was left with approximately one thousand dollars and was criticized by relatives and friends when she insisted on tithing it, giving a hundred dollars to the church. She divided all her belongings between the two stepchildren, Newland and Irene, keeping only her clothing and a few personal effects. Newland was marrying a California girl and Irene wanted to live with her aunts in California.

Soon after, Willie Mae decided to return to Texas and live in Waxahachie with her parents. She packed her few belongings and got on the train with Billy. He never forgot the day they arrived there. It was a hot day of a sort with which not even Bakersfield could compete. Billy and his mother walked from the depot, eventually turning up the dusty little road where his grandfather's furniture store was located. Ahead of them he saw an old man walking steadily along.

"That's your grandfather," his mother said. "Run and catch him!"

Billy ran as fast as his little legs could carry him. He grabbed and hugged around the knees this new person in his life, his really truly grandfather. But, oh, how very old he looked!

The old man reached down to pick Billy up and press him in a hug. There among the whiskers was Billy's introduction to life in Waxahachie, Texas.

Billy Roberts and his mother were welcomed into her parents' home. He felt uprooted from all things near and dear to him.

His grandparents were loving and kind, as were his mother's younger sisters, still at home. But it was a strange world and he began to withdraw into a world of make-believe. He was not a very well-behaved little boy. Being naughty attracted attention, which he greatly desired.

Soon after returning to Waxahachie, a younger brother, Thomas Allen Roberts, was born. Rather then becoming jealous, Billy wanted to be a real big brother to him.

Willie Mae was determined that she would bring up her son Billy " . . . in the nurture and admonition of the Lord" (Ephesians 6:4). At that time, tent meetings and evangelistic services in various churches of the town occurred frequently. Women and children were safe on the streets at night and Willie Mae took Billy by the hand and walked to many of them. He liked the tent meetings, where the histrionic fireworks appealed to his sense of the dramatic. Next morning, Billy would stand before the mirror, faithfully recreating each movement and gesture, and in *sotto voce* mimicking each unctuous phrase. He was disinterested in what the speakers said, only how they said it.

Although his mother was a stabilizing Christian influence on his life, she really didn't get through to Billy at all. She'd bring him to her knee while she read passages from the Bible, but his mind would wander far away. Often when she came in to his bedside to pray he'd pretend to be asleep. His mother memorized a lot of verses from her well-worn Bible and some of these he remembered quite well. These were the unpleasant verses, which were impressed upon his mind by way of his little bottom.

By the time Billy was eleven or twelve, he already had

experience as an amateur entertainer of children and also adults. He did recitations, skits and impersonations with considerable skill for a boy who was completely innocent of any training. A drama teacher who had a radio program in Dallas had Bill audition for her. She was so impressed with his talent she had him mow her lawn and do odd jobs to pay for drama lessons.

During Bill's high-school years, he got a part-time job taking tickets at the local movie houses. These show people seemed to be living such marvelous and happy lives. Acting was Bill's whole world and he worked at it diligently for hours at a time. In high-school assemblies he was called upon to act out some of his plays as well as recitals in large auditoriums. All of this allowed him to merge all his yearnings for the theatrical world.

One Sunday morning at church when they were singing the invitation hymn, he walked down the aisle. A number of little old ladies wept. When the pastor asked if he had received Jesus, he gave the right answer to that and the other questions. After all, he'd grown up in Sunday school there.

That night he was baptized and received into the fellowship of the church, everything correct and entered on the church rolls. But his responses had been superficial. He just went through the motions and in his own opinion it was a pretty poor act. He didn't remember it as a blessing at all. Taking off his wet clothing with the other men after immersion embarrassed him. It was like the locker room at school. He didn't like it and was not really born again. Instead, he was to go out and live for the devil for a number of years. He had merely done what was expected of him.

When Bill was seventeen, he was graduated from high school. He felt a deep desire to go on to college and get a degree, though if asked exactly why, he'd have been hard put to give the reasons, and financial help from his people was an impossibility.

About graduation time the navy recruiting posters at the post office suggested a possible answer to his problem. The navy fed you, housed you, trained you and gave pay you could save for college.

In a happy mood, Bill made an entrance through the kitchen door and announced, "Mother, I'm going to join the navy!"

His mother looked him right in the eye. "No, you're not! You're still a minor. You can't join unless I give my signed consent."

"But, Mother, I've already passed my physical. This is what I really want to do now." He argued until she gave in, insisting, however, on going to the recruiting office with him before signing anything.

At the recruiting office, Bill's mother came face-to-face with a grizzled old chief wearing the eagle with gold chevrons and hash marks the whole length of his sleeve. The chief returned her gaze steadily as she moved up to point-blank range.

"Mister," she began, "do they feed the boys well in the navy?"

The chief liked that one. "Lady, navy chow is famous all over the world. There's none better, not even home cooking—begging your pardon."

"Good beds and clean clothing?"

"That's right. Don't you worry, M'am."

After more of such questions, all answered very posi-
tively, there was a long silence. Pen in hand, her voice
quivering with intensity, she said, "I'm sending a very fine
boy to the navy and I want your solemn promise you'll
send him back just as fine a boy."

The chief promised and she signed the papers. After
that, she left very quickly, as a wounded person rushes
forward before falling.

Bill was not allowed to leave the office. He was sworn
in with a group of other recruits. That same day they were
put on a train for San Diego and boot camp at the naval
training station.

2

Boot camp completed, his traveling orders were issued for an assignment in the Aleutian chain. Bill found life as a storekeeper in the Kodiak commissary store boring and he was miserable much of the eighteen months he served on Kodiak Island.

At the end of his two-year navy obligation, Bill returned to Waxahachie, Texas, and continued his high-school romance with his girl friend, Ramona. That summer they talked about future plans and both decided to attend the University of Texas at Austin.

Bill soon discovered just how seriously distressed Ramona's parents were about their interest in each other. Fearing an elopement, they acted swiftly. Her college registration was changed from the University of Texas to Wayland College, a small Baptist co-ed college in Plainview, Texas. Thus torn apart, the two young lovers were heartbroken. But Ramona soon changed and wrote to tell him of her love for someone else.

Bill's perfunctory stand for the Lord Jesus at age sixteen meant almost nothing to him now. God was remembered only in times of serious trouble. The change in Ramona gave Bill further excuse for bitterness and resentment.

Then a remarkable man came into Bill's life. He was B. Iden Payne, one of the top Shakespearean directors in the world. He had directed more Shakespeare than any living man. He had been director of the Stratford-on-Avon Theater in England. He had directed both Ethel Barrymore and Helen Hayes on Broadway. Getting older now, he was devoting his life to teaching Shakespearean drama. To be a student of B. Iden Payne was a rare privilege; he had so much to offer. He fairly lived and breathed Shakespearean plays and didn't even need scripts for most of them. Knowing them word for word, he gave them life.

B. Iden Payne was a turning point in Bill Roberts's life. Here was a man who represented excellence in his field. He knew intimately the works of the world's greatest playwright. He had worked and studied in the place of his birth. He had directed this century's finest performers of Shakespeare on the most prestigious stages of America. Having the simple confidence of a master, he was kind, helpful and sympathetic to any student genuinely attracted to that art which was his life.

With the steady encouragement of this gifted man, Bill Roberts began to develop his natural talent for drama. He worked hard and played good parts in a number of Shakespearean plays. He became an assistant director, one of whose duties was to cue in a person saying a wrong line. Usually, before Bill could do so, Mr. Payne would correct from memory.

Midway in his senior year at college, lacking just one semester of getting his degree, Bill was faced with a decision. His financial assistance on the G.I. Bill was running out. Somehow he would need to earn the money to finance the last months before graduation.

Just then, Burl Cass, one of the drama teachers and directors, had visions of a repertory company that would travel extensively and he asked Bill to join up. It seemed that this company could grow into a very big thing. They were to sign contracts and be paid regular salaries. Cass hired an advance man and chose a number of excellent actors and actresses. Bill was one of the youngest members of the troupe.

Feeling that this was the opportunity of a lifetime to get actual professional training and experience, Bill flung himself into exhausting rehearsals. He played everything from Baptista in *Taming of the Shrew,* to Banquo in *Macbeth,* Starveling in *Midsummer Night's Dream* and Will Scarlet in a very flashy production of *Robin Hood* for children's audiences.

This was not a company with a great deal of money and out on the road they did not live glamorously. But Bill was learning a great deal about acting and more than a little about the life of an actor on the road. Sometimes the advance man had done poorly and sparse audiences resulted. At other times, particularly in larger cities where the publicity had been good, they played before thousands in a night. They had to adjust daily from situations like playing in the gym of a small high school with makeshift facilities to beautiful theaters with every modern convenience. While Bill was playing his various roles, he was also learning the parts of other leads, just from hearing them over and over. It was an unusual opportunity to pick up tricks

of the trade by being involved with more experienced
performers.

Nevertheless Bill felt frustrated and far from satisfied
with his present life. The enthusiasm with which he had
jumped at a chance with the troupe was wearing thin. He
had soon learned about all that this sort of experience
could teach. His goal of the Broadway stage seemed far-off
and out of reach. Besides this, he was aware from time to
time of a sense of dissatisfaction with Bill Roberts as a
person. He knew that his mother was praying for him day
and night. He had never wanted to hurt her and at times
he had deep pangs of conscience, but they didn't cut
deeply enough for repentance and a turning away from
the kind of life he was living. All that would have to wait
for a more convenient day.

The drama company remained on tour for several
months. Financial returns were much less than expected.

Touring with this troupe, Bill did learn other skills besides survival without money. There was a difference between the careful preparation for a play at Austin and the
rapid preparation, rehearsal and plunging into a production which were now a part of his everyday life. A quick
study, the lines came easily to Bill, allowing him to concentrate on important details whose mastery made the
difference between a good and an outstanding actor.

Before the tour was completed, Burl Cass unexpectedly
arrived to announce that the company had run out of
money. There'd been complications with the advance
man and other problems. He couldn't see any possibility
of going on with the show.

Instead of arriving in Dallas in great glory, they folded in Dallas. Bill was stranded with barely enough money to buy a bus ticket back to Waxahachie.

Bill's mother was delighted to have him back again. She thought it was time he settled down to a normal life close to home.

To her, a normal life meant getting a decent job so he could marry a nice local girl and start raising a family. Bill was far from delighted. Three times he'd tried to escape from Waxahachie, and here he was, back in the same old rut with no way out in sight.

Bill couldn't find a conventional job in either Waxahachie or in Dallas. It seemed that a college major in drama was not a prerequisite for many jobs. He lacked the experience and training for what few jobs opened up at the time.

Then he learned that the Arthur Murray School of Dancing needed instructors. The training was free to those who were accepted; the student instructor, however, had to provide his own room and board. Bill was accepted and placed in a training class—eight hours a day for eight weeks. He felt that they were dancing him to death. At the end of each day, he crawled into bed, one aching lump of misery. Boot camp was nothing like this. However, he did have a natural aptitude for dancing and enjoyed it and became a top instructor.

One thing kept Bill going: Arthur Murray had studios all over the country, especially in New York City. He would do so well in Dallas that he'd have a chance to transfer to New York. Then he could eat while he became known to the casting directors. The hours at Murray's were flexible enough so that he could keep any theatrical casting appointment that might open up to him. First Dallas, then New York; that was his plan.

He said to his manager, "Boy! If I could work in New York for a while, I'd come back here a better dance instructor. Those New York studios have more prestige than any of the others. Why, the Murrays themselves manage one and Mrs. Murray's brother manages another."

"I know all that, but you're much better off running your own place."

"But. . . ."

Bill finally got his transfer and bought a one-way ticket to New York. He went home to Waxahachie and announced, "Mother, I'm going to New York City. At last I'm going to the city I've dreamed about for half my life."

Bill knew that somehow he was going to make it on his own. He got off the bus at Thirty-Fourth Street, asked if there was a YMCA nearby and somebody pointed out one down the street.

After getting settled, Bill—dressed in his best, a twenty-eight-dollar suit with loud checks—walked through the door of Arthur Murray's exclusive studio and presented himself as the new dance instructor. He could sense that they were looking him over critically. It would have been a comfort had he realized how many smart-looking New Yorkers had first come to the place from some small town, wearing a cheap suit and an expression of bewilderment.

The criterion at Murray's was whether he could do the job successfully.

Bill was accepted, but this did not mean full-time work at once. It was not their policy to take pupils away from any of their staff to give work to a new instructor. Bill would have to build up his own clientele. They gave him some of the new students and some of those returning after an absence for more lessons. He was paid by the hour —very small amounts the first few weeks—but with his eight-dollar room, a few hot dogs and delicatessen snacks, he was able to eke out a meager existence.

At last, Bill Roberts was in New York, the city of his dreams. A good, brisk walk would take him to Broadway, yet sometimes, as he lay on his musty bed, the bright lights and the stages he yearned for seemed as far away as Kodiak and as much of a dream as when he performed for the chickens, way back there in his Waxahachie childhood.

3

While working part-time at Arthur Murray's, Bill developed twin boils in his middle ear. Soon he was sick with pain—hardly able to think of anything else. He still had very little money and didn't know a doctor who might treat him on credit.

Among Bill's students at the time was a shy little lady named Katherine Miles, whose husband had left her for a younger woman. Her sincerity and gentle good manners appealed to Bill and he did everything he could to draw her out of herself. When he introduced her to other people, he'd find her almost behind him, hands trembling from fear. None of the other instructors cared to bother with her, but Bill found her a challenge. Kindliness shone gently through her timid smile and he became determined to draw her out and give her back a measure of the self-confidence she had lost—perhaps never really had.

Naturally this lady took in Bill's twenty-eight-dollar suit, the inexpensive shirts and ties, the scuffed shoes no polish would restore. Very well dressed in a quiet way, she obviously knew good clothes from cheap.

Bill dragged himself to the studio that day and she happened to be the pupil. Noticing his swollen cheek and inflamed ear, she was distressed and compassionate. Relationship between pupil and instructor at Murray's was strictly formal: instructors were to be addressed as Mr. or Miss, as the case might be. After they had danced a little while, she said, "Let's sit this one out. You don't feel like dancing today."

She said it so nicely, and knowing that she understood, he sank down gratefully into a chair beside her. Then she said, "Mr. Roberts, please don't be embarrassed. You need medical help with that dreadful boil. We both understand that you're new here and you can't have been making much. Now please . . . I'd like to help you go to a doctor." Then she slipped him several ten dollar bills, doing it so that nobody would notice.

Her genuine concern, expressed in that shy and gentle way she had, made it seem perfectly aboveboard. Very gratefully, Bill accepted her gift and found a doctor to lance his boils.

Eventually, Katherine Miles became a beautiful dancer. Gradually she gained in self-confidence and poise, revealing stronger facets of her personality which had been inhibited during her unhappy marriage. She had a lifetime course, which at Arthur Murray's meant one thousand hours of instruction paid in advance. Before long, Bill was teaching six lifetime members. One of these was on her third lifetime course. She'd spent thirty-two thousand dollars on dance lessons, and if she could do nothing else in life, at least was a fabulous dancer.

Bill had arrived at Murray's in August. As the months went by, he began to really enjoy teaching little Mrs.

Miles, but he never forgot his principal motivation—a career in acting.

Although his decorous friendship with Katherine Miles had grown steadily, she didn't offer to do anything for him until the Christmas holidays approached. Then she said, "Mr. Roberts, wouldn't you like to spend Christmas with your family in Texas?"

"Oh, I'd love to see them, Mrs. Miles. There's so much to tell them about what's happened here."

"Well, I'd like to give you a little Christmas gift—a round-trip ticket home."

As Bill stammered his thanks, he thought, It's a good thing she said *round*-trip.

She raised a hand to cut him short and said, "Mr. Roberts, I—you'll need some new clothes for your trip home."

She took him to one of the most exclusive stores in New York. They sold Louis Roth suits—beautiful stuff he'd never have dared to ask about on his own. Even in those days the suits were priced from a hundred and fifty to something like three hundred fifty dollars and everything else priced in proportion. While his mouth gaped with astonishment and his eyes shone his delight, she bought Bill a suit, a sport coat, two pairs of slacks, a gold vest, a cashmere overcoat and all the accessories. He went to choose these beautiful clothes in his twenty-eight-dollar suit, now threadbare and sagging out of shape. Then into his hand she pressed a round-trip ticket to Dallas and some spending money.

Bill's mother and some relatives had come to pick him up. His mother was looking for his face. What he might be wearing was of no moment to her. Bill was thinking, I left on a bus and now I come home very glamorously. This is real living! Even as he walked toward his mother, he was thinking, It'll be like this all the time when I'm famous in show business.

His mother was not excited about the progress he thought he was making in the world. She didn't even seem impressed with his beautiful clothes. She quoted every Bible verse she had ever memorized. And it was by no accident, Bill was sure, that the pastor visited several times.

When time came to leave, his mother cried and he felt sorry for her.

Bill went back to New York City—back to Murray's to teach there for a few more months. In his spare time he kept making the rounds of the theaters. Then he read that Tennessee Williams was doing a revival of *Streetcar Named Desire*. Mr. Williams was casting the show himself! Bill thought he could play the part of the newsboy who did the love scene with Blanche. Just to be in a Tennessee Williams show that the playwright was casting himself would be a tremendous boost toward his career as an actor.

This was an off-Broadway theater. The producer said to Bill, "You're absolutely perfect for the show that's now running. Can you learn a part in three days? We have an emergency casting."

Bill said, "Sure, I can." He hadn't seen the part. It was the part of an emotionally upset young fellow and perhaps they thought he was a perfect typecasting. He wouldn't even have to work up a characterization. The part was him.

The name of the show was *The Chair*, a psychological drama by a playwright named Thomas Hill. It had been running quite a number of months, was no great hit and could close any day. But Bill had been offered the juvenile lead.

That evening, Bill went back to his job at Arthur Murray's in a troubled state of mind. The chance on the stage he had been waiting for so eagerly had suddenly been offered to him, but to accept meant leaving his steady job in three days without giving proper notice. They would never take him back. The acting part offered him opportunity without security. Within days—a few weeks at most —that show would close, and the casting for the Williams play was now complete. A decision had to be made.

He danced with his favorite pupil that night, little Katherine Miles. He told her about the break he'd been offered —the one she knew he'd been waiting for. In his anxiety over making a decision, he became quite negative. He could be out on the street within a week: no pay check, no money for rent or food. The more he talked about it, the more anxious he became. His vivid imagination could always be trusted to conjure up horrible things happening in any unknown circumstance.

Before he had finished his recitation of lurking disaster, she put her hand on his arm and stopped him. "Mr. Roberts, I've been thinking it over as we've been dancing. I really think you should take that part—I have a lot of faith in you as a person—as an actor. I hate to lose you as a teacher, but I—I believe you're going to do very well on the stage. Someday your name will be known just like the others."

He knew what she meant—maybe not a Brando, but his name could be there in lights on Broadway. He knew he could do it.

Then despair flooded over him again, "But there's no way. . . ."

"Mr. Roberts, I'd like to help you. I want to help you. Here's your chance; take it. Soon enough you won't need help from anybody." Her mouth twisted in a strange little smile and he noticed that she was wadding her handkerchief with both hands in her lap. "I'd like to be the one who gave you that little boost on your way to success."

Bill thanked her, oh, how he thanked her! He could reach for his dream without fear. Nothing would stop him now.

Murray's were quite decent about letting him go, but there was a polite finality terminating their relationship when he was given his pay. Prospective branch managers don't walk out of Murray's like that and expect to return when they need a job. Bill sensed this, but his euphoria quickly pushed anxieties of any kind from his mind.

The envy of his friends, he moved from his little broom closet of a room to an airy, spacious one. It never occurred to him that he was entering into a life of subtle bondage.

He went back to the theater and got the part. The director blocked him in without the other actors being present. With only three days to prepare, he took pills to stay awake at night and learn his lines.

On a Saturday night, he opened to a packed house. Waiting in the wings for his cue to come on, he thought that he would die. Fear gripped him; he couldn't remember a line. He was an unknown; nobody on either side of the lights knew him. How they'd laugh if he blew it! He'd be a flop in his first chance and end his stage career before it got started.

There had been someone in the audience who knew him: Katherine Miles, who had made all this possible. Off-Broadway didn't pay much, but it was the wedge to open the big doors of opportunity, and it was also a wonderful school. Bill's sponsor was shy, but she knew the ropes around show business. Bit by bit, she encouraged Bill in getting to be known. His wardrobe continued to grow with two-hundred-fifty-dollar suits and other very expensive clothes. He was usually better dressed than the producers and directors of the plays he did. Superficially —in appearance and manner—he developed an air of confident self-assurance.

Bill began to study with some of the finest professional acting teachers in New York—Tony Manino, Uta Hagen, Lee Grant and others. He had the advantage of nearly four years majoring in drama at the University of Texas. His field had been acting and now he was beginning to work with people who were doing shows on Broadway, among them Steve McQueen, Sandy Dennis, James Garner and Fritzie Burr. His fellow students were professional people, many of them already embarked on brilliant careers on stage and screen.

Summer came and Bill's younger brother, Tommy, was being graduated from high school. Katherine Miles asked him, "Why don't you fly to your brother's graduation?" He flew home for the occasion. A few months later, she said, "Why don't you ask your mother and your brother if they'd like a trip to New York? They've never been here."

Bill wrote an invitation and they came, not realizing at the time who was paying all the expenses.

His sponsor said, "You need a bigger place now that they're coming." So he got a beautiful apartment in the Turtle Bay area close to Katherine Hepburn's place. It seemed to Bill that his feet hardly touched the pavement all the rest of that day, so glowing was his euphoria. He was really going places now! It didn't occur to him that this lovely place to live and to receive his mother had been handed to him gift wrapped. It was all very simple. He had talent and the beginnings of success were sweet. He looked forward to this visit with his mother and his brother, yet when they came, they seemed quite casual about his success. Tommy was pleased, though not excited. He said calmly that it was sure different from Texas. The worst of it was his mother's attitude. It was negative. She didn't seem to like New York very much. She fell asleep during the first act of a play he'd selected as certain to delight her. She asked too many questions about how much the theater paid him and how much rent he paid. She agreed that his clothes were nice, but her mind seemed on other things. She asked where he went to church and he didn't do very well answering that one.

Then came the deluge of Bible verses. It was with relief that he saw them off for Dallas and home. They were his people, but somehow he felt so awkward when they were around his New York friends.

Bill had grown beyond being embarrassed about spending money he hadn't earned. He was doing good things with it, he told himself—like sending money home to his mother and helping his brother through college.

There in New York, one show led to another. He began to be known as a working actor. Between plays, he escorted his sponsor to the Waldorf and the Plaza. Katherine was petite, and because of her dancing ability and their similarity in appearance, was often mistaken for Mrs. Arthur Murray. The big-name orchestra leaders came to know them and would call Bill up and ask, "What would you like us to play?"

They loved the Latin dances, tangos, rumbas and sambas. Often the crowd cleared the dance floor while the two of them performed what amounted to exhibition dances—the sort of things they had done at the awards balls in the Arthur Murray days. Katherine drank in the applause, for it was the first real recognition she had ever received in her empty life. Now that she was going to the theater to see Bill act, or going with him to other performances, they began to frequent the top restaurants in New York. Cocktails and fine wines with their meals, tips and taxicabs—these became everyday matters to Bill. His sponsor lavished upon him what shortly before would have seemed a fortune. From time to time she gave him great rolls of money to spend as he pleased.

In order to give more attractive parties, Bill moved again. He sublet the apartment in the Turtle Bay area and found a ground-floor apartment in a brownstone located in the East Seventies, near Park Avenue, with people like Henry Fonda and Kim Novak as neighbors.

Things had become much too easy for Bill. In his foolish egoism, he turned down opportunities that would have furthered his career. After something like a year on the New York stage, he was offered an apprentice acting job with an outstanding company to play the entire summer. He would have excellent supporting roles working with well-known stars. Here was a chance to advance his ability and his reputation. Although he had been taught that an actor should accept all sorts of roles for the experience and also be seen by the widest possible audience, Bill had begun to think that he should take nothing but the better leads. His wealthy little sponsor had been pushing him ahead much too fast for his own good. The glamour of night life was becoming so exciting that he didn't want to leave New York for the summer. When the contract was brought to him in person for his signature, he refused it.

Bill auditioned for Joseph Papp and his director, Stuart Vaughn. Joseph Papp, now fifty-one, has been a driving force in New York theater. For sixteen years, his free, open-air Shakespeare in Central Park has been internationally famous. After creating New York's Public Theater, he now has charge of the prestigious Lincoln Center.

After a successful audition, Bill was accepted and did two shows for Papp. From there he went on to the Cherry Lane theater, where he did two shows, including *Camille,* with Colleen Dewhurst. This was an important experience for him as Dewhurst was an outstanding actress with a record of great roles equaled by few.

After this start it was relatively easy to keep working. Bill decided to try out for summer stock. Most actors, excepting the well-established stars, like to do this, not only for the extra money, but for the variety of experience in different roles which summer stock offers.

He found that it was a memorable summer experience.

Back in New York, he continued to study and to look for work. Katherine Miles, his sponsor, urged him to relax.

"You must rest, dear boy. You've had a very difficult summer."

"But I'm between shows. I've got to find a job—do something to earn some money."

"No, Bill." She put a hand on his arm, very gently, yet almost with an air of authority. "Oh, no, you can't do that. You must be available for the theater."

"But I need the money." Bill was wrestling with the natural desire to be independent and the inclination to just let matters slide a little longer until he was really established in the theater.

"Money's no problem. Here. . . ." She opened her purse as she so often did, as if that expensive little bag held all the answers to his problems. "You never have to work at anything again except a suitable part in the theater."

So he began to live like a young millionaire playboy. Between shows she kept showering him with expensive clothes, valuable little personal gifts and always a wad of money when she thought he could use it.

But it was not a free life. There was a regular routine of seeing Katherine every Wednesday night and every Saturday night that he was not in a show. On these nights he had the definite obligation of escorting her out to dinner and then on to either the theater or an evening of dancing. These were times of keen frustration for Bill. He was in his early twenties and he'd meet girls that he was interested in. If they liked each other, eventually it would get around to, "What shall we do?" Most of the girls would say, "Why don't we do something Saturday night?" Then they would begin to wonder what there was in his life that he never could go anywhere on Saturday and sometimes Wednesday evenings.

Bill began to see glimpses of Katherine's deep jealousy. After one of her cutting remarks, Bill burst out with, "You want to own me, don't you?"

And she said, "Yes."

He said, "Nobody will ever own me!" He said it with great dramatic effect, but he knew that she spoke the truth. She ruined every promising relationship with any girl he wanted as a friend. They were either hurt, or confused, or scornfully angry, according to their understanding of such relationships. There were fellows Bill knew who thought him a smart and clever operator. Some of them were deeply involved with older women, and for a lot less than he was having done for him. But despite personal frustration, Bill's stage career was prospering.

Bill had always sent his mother money from time to time. Now he wanted her to come to New York for a good visit. He wanted to really show her the city; there had been so little time when she'd come with Tommy. His mother didn't seem to enjoy New York much that time. This visit would be different, he was sure. When she showed real interest in coming, he was delighted.

When Bill met the plane, he was struck all over again at how pretty she looked. She was now in her middle fifties, a trifle plump, but always neat and careful of her appearance. She had brought some lovely clothes to wear —her sister Virginia had a dress shop and had enjoyed helping her get ready for New York.

Bill felt that he was taking her everywhere in New York. Everywhere to him meant the world of the theater. He took her to a number of performances, and one night to a very funny Broadway show. It was a rerun of her first visit. About the middle of the second act he felt something heavy against his shoulder. His mother had gone to sleep on him again.

He still didn't realize that she'd come to New York, not to see the town, but to reach him. She didn't say so, but she felt at the time that she'd just met the biggest phony of her whole life: her own son, Bill. She knew how to deflate him, and she did—right in front of those people who mattered to him until he was ready to crawl under a table and hide.

She came for two weeks and stayed eleven. He thought she would never go home. There were forces fighting within him, nearly tearing him apart. He knew the side he was on and he knew that she was on the other side and that she was really stronger than he was because she was

there to remind her son about the Lord Jesus Christ. And
that was the last subject he wanted to discuss at the time.

The pressures pushed Bill from both sides and he nearly
had what people call a nervous breakdown. At the time,
he was in rehearsal for one of the shows with Joseph Papp,
which was important to his career, yet he was so upset
that he begged to get out of it.

Joseph Papp said, "This is a very unprofessional attitude
you're taking, Bill—asking to be released when we're
ready to go into production. Your costumes are already
made, you know the part and it could be very important
to you. I can't have this production fall apart now."

Papp talked him out of quitting and Bill went on to do
the part. He did his best, but he was so distraught, he
could not concentrate sufficiently to throw himself into it.
One side of him was trying to be an actor, but the real Bill
Roberts was being pulled apart by two women, his mother
and Katherine Miles.

4

Bill's mother met his sponsor, Katherine Miles, and the two of them entered into undeclared warfare over his body and soul. Katherine Miles was older than his mother, yet she made a point of addressing her as Mrs. Roberts in a tone of voice just a shade short of being respectful, as if to imply, You might just as well think of yourself as an old woman, my dear.

Willie Mae Roberts had been outspoken all her life. Now she struggled for self-control. What mattered to her was Bill. This woman and all the rest of what she saw happening were destroying her son.

"Billy, will you please come back to Texas before it's too late? Won't you give up this theater business before it destroys you completely? Won't you leave this kind of life with these fake friends of yours? And Bill, won't you commit your life to Jesus Christ? He could bring you real success and real peace."

He grew angry and said, "Mother, don't you ever suggest my giving up the theater. Theater is my life! Theater is my god!"

"The Bible says, 'Thou shalt have no other gods before me.' "

"But Mother. . . ."

"You can try to have other gods, but they'll crumble into nothing. The only safe place for things we love is under His protection."

"I'm not giving up the theater for anybody—not for you and not for God either!"

His mother's face had turned pale as he talked. In a little while, when she could compose herself, she said, "Bill, please make reservations. I'm going home."

He was glad she was going home. He made reservations for her the next day and took her to the airport. He watched a brokenhearted woman start walking toward the plane. Halfway up the steps, she stopped—and stopped everybody behind her as she turned and gazed at Bill once more with a look that he would never forget.

During this period, Bill had quite a few good offers. He was asked again to play lesser roles in a star company and at the same time was asked to play the leads in the Gateway Theater in Bellport, Long Island. He auditioned, was accepted and signed a contract with Equity, to play the lead in *Will Success Spoil Rock Hunter?* the young male lead in *Witness for the Prosecution* and in some of the top shows that had been recent Broadway hits.

He had two weeks to himself before going to Long Island for rehearsal of the first of ten shows. During this time, he changed his stage name to Robert Dayton because Equity had another actor under contract also named Bill Roberts.

During these two weeks something happened to the Bill Roberts from Waxahachie. Following the Ringling

Brothers' Circus, the evangelist, Billy Graham, came to Madison Square Garden. There was much apprehension that he would flop in New York. No evangelist could hold a crowd in a cynical place that had seen them all come and seen them all go.

Bill's curiosity got the better of him. This man must be a splendid actor. He really should go and watch his technique. Perhaps he could pick up a few little tricks that would be useful in the theater. Of course, his mother had written and though he didn't know it at the time, she had stirred a regular hornet's nest of prayer rising out of Waxahachie. It was the technique, the stage presence he was going to see. After all, the theater was his god.

On May 28, 1957, Bill walked up to Madison Square Garden. The only seat he could find was at the back of the third gallery. Used to nothing but the very best seats in restaurants and theaters, he didn't like this seat in the peanut gallery. All about him people looked at him and smiled as if sharing their happy anticipation of a memorable event, so he sat down without grumbling.

When Billy Graham came out, Bill was ready for him, meaning to be critical, to judge him. But right away, he knew deep in his heart that this man was on the level and believed every word he was saying. One phrase he used constantly really struck Bill head on: "The Bible says . . . ." He held his open Bible in his hands and started quoting Bible verses. "Therefore if any man be in Christ, he is a new creature: old things are passed away; behold, all things are become new" (2 Corinthians 5:17). Bill knew about Jesus Christ in his head, but he didn't know Him personally and he certainly wasn't living "in Christ." Billy Graham was quoting so many verses that had a familiar ring, yet they had never struck Bill with such power. He felt thrust back into his seat until he ached from the tension of holding his body so rigidly.

Bill gave up trying to argue with the speaker. He was scarcely aware of others in that huge crowd. This man had got to him—was describing the miserable and unfulfilled life of Bill Roberts. It was no use trying to kid himself. New York hadn't been all that great. Each little gain in the theater had come at a high price, and the life he was now living was a half life—everything beyond the footlights unfulfilled hunger and emptiness. Troubled muddy water —really much of his life was like that. He didn't feel clean, and he hadn't known a day of peace for years.

Billy Graham quoted from the Bible again, then he said, "God forgives and forgets. He washes us clean and we are clothed with His righteousness."

There was a great deal more and then he came to the end of his message and Bill, squirming and sweating, was glad of that. But now it seemed to Bill the speaker said an amazing thing. "You may be in show business—seeking fame and fortune. You may be named Bill, Jim, John, Mary. Fame and fortune cannot save you. There's only one way. Jesus said 'I am the way, the truth, and the life: no man cometh unto the Father but by me' " (John 14:6).

Bill knew the man was talking to him as if they were alone somewhere. He had always thought there were a dozen ways to God, a sort of self-improvement proposition.

Bill Roberts had no idea what Billy Graham would do at the end of his message. He did what he *always* does. He looked all around that great auditorium and said, "Now I want you to stand up and step out and walk down these aisles and stand here in front as an indication that you are committing your life to Jesus Christ. Walking down that aisle won't save your soul, and you're not coming to Billy Graham. You receive Christ by faith and then, stepping out and coming down here you are publicly recognizing Him as your Saviour. . . . Hundreds are coming already. If you feel this need in your life, *you come.*"

When the challenge seemed to be over, Bill quit squirming low in his seat and took a deep breath. Then he saw Billy Graham's finger pointed right at him as he said, "You still have time to give your life to Jesus Christ, but come right now."

Bill stood up. All of a sudden he didn't care anymore that eighteen thousand people were staring at him. He got into that back passageway and ran down three flights of steps, just in time to join the crowd that had been standing in front and now headed for the basement for counseling. A mechanic with work-stained hands and a tattered Bible followed Bill and took him over. This man knew nothing about the stage as Bill knew nothing about things mechanical, but his new friend knew Jesus Christ. When they sat down together, he asked Bill a number of questions, gave him a number of verses, a small packet of Navigators' material and then prayed a simple prayer. Later he wrote Bill a number of follow-up letters to see how he was doing. As he said good-bye the man gripped

Bill's hand warmly and said, "You've been born again tonight, Bill. You'll never be sorry."

Bill left Madison Square Garden feeling really clean for the first time in years. For the first time in his life, he was able to talk about Jesus without embarrassment. He thought, This is like when a person falls in love with someone, it's so natural and easy to say His name and tell people about the One who means so much to me. Jesus has loved me all this time before I really considered wanting to love Him back!

That night he put in a long-distance call to Waxahachie and told his mother exactly what had happened to him. She said, "Oh, Bill! I could die happy tonight! I'd almost given up on you!"

Bill didn't feel that she had ever given up on him. For almost twenty-eight years she had prayed for this night.

5

Bill awoke the next morning flooded with euphoria. He had not yet had time to sort out his thoughts or to consider the full meaning of the repentance he had expressed when he had accepted Christ the night before. He was so happy—filled with a new sense of joy, peace and release from fear. "Jesus, You're wonderful!" he said softly. He knew that some hard answers needed to be given to questions raised the night before in Madison Square Garden, but he pushed all that to the back of his mind. Right now, he just wanted to enjoy his happiness.

This was a Wednesday. As he was not working, he was obligated to spend the evening with Katherine Miles. The designated meeting place was at an intersection not far from the Garden. He approached with a full heart, bursting with desire to share his experience with her. When still more than a block away, he saw her waiting for him. Unaware of his approach, she was smoking a cigarette, inhaling deeply as she swung impatiently back and forth, grinding a heel on the pavement. For the first time in his life, he saw her with eyes that were no longer veiled. She was his jailer. He lived in a well-furnished prison and as a pampered prisoner he'd been wasting his life for years.

Something had to change.

They went to dinner as usual and all during the meal—in great excitement—he shared with her his good news and the joy which flooded his heart. Verses Billy Graham had quoted, which Bill had learned as a child, now began to pour out of him as though they had never lain dormant. There was a light in his eyes she had never seen before as he stumbled over words trying to give the dimensions of his new experience.

All the time he was talking, Bill was watching her face. First there was a look of incredulity, then of chilly negation. She couldn't understand his enthusiasm; she put the whole experience in the light of his having gone to a rather poor show.

Bill said, "Katherine, won't you come to the Garden with me tonight and hear Billy Graham? This man is for real, and what's a lot more important, Jesus Christ is real!" Then he blurted out, "You can find Him too. He can change your whole life. You really haven't any idea what . . . ."

She cut him off. He noticed that her mouth was rather ugly as she said with cold finality, "Don't get any stupid ideas like that. I'm not going there with you or anybody —not tonight or ever. Bill, you've been worrying about your career and you haven't been yourself recently. Why don't you go to a really good psychiatrist. . . ."

This time Bill broke in. "Katherine, believe me, I went to the right doctor last night—and I found the exactly right—the perfect cure for my problem. It's Jesus. He's the One. I wish I could explain. . . ."

His evenings with Katherine Miles were a strain on both of them. She was trying to be patient with him until he recovered from his binge with "old-time religion" that spoiled everything. By now she was eager for him to go to Long Island and get involved in playing leads in summer stock. Even if he was a quick study, learning a lead part every week would keep his mind occupied and she hoped that he'd soon be himself again.

The time arrived for rehearsals. Bill arrived at Bellport, Long Island, in a sleek new convertible, bringing a Billy Graham songbook and his new Bible. His roommate was Gene Hackman, now a star in Hollywood. Robert Duvall, now well known in motion pictures and on TV, was also in the company.

He began to get up early in the morning because Billy Graham and other Christians he'd met said that it was wonderful to meet the Lord in the morning for devotions. His roommate, Gene Hackman, was a very nice guy and Bill didn't want to disturb him. So early in the morning he would slip quietly out of bed without turning on a light. He'd go over by the window and watch the dawn. Then by the light of the rising sun, he would read his Bible. During this time, he read the Gospel of John over six times.

The first production (and the one in which Bill played the young male lead) was *Witness for the Prosecution*. He began to believe that God had arranged the time and place of this play and his part in it. The play was about a young married man who was involved with an older woman—mostly for her money. He has killed her and is on trial for his life. His wife stands by him all the way, believing him innocent. He is declared innocent by the jury, but only after the shocking revelation that he's had another girl on the side who gave him a firm alibi. Innocent in the eyes of the law and guilty in the eyes of God, he stands with the younger girl in his arms—and his wife stabs him to death. Some of this young man's speeches paralleled the feeling Bill had and it sickened him.

One day, two student actresses (who had a mild crush on Bill) happened to come by and asked what he was reading.

"The Bible," he said, and shared his new faith with them. A day or so later both of them appeared with Bibles and asked his help in exploring what to them was a deep mystery. Their interest seemed genuine and he encouraged them to keep on reading God's Word. (Later on, after her return to New York, one girl went to one of the meetings at Madison Square Garden and accepted Christ.)

Soon, Bill realized that he must surrender everything to Jesus. The biggest thing in his life was his acting career. Racked with sobs, he yielded this area of his life to Jesus Christ.

He said aloud, "Lord Jesus, I give you my life—my acting career, my future in the theater. Whatever You want, I'm willing to do."

That night, the audience reacted very warmly to the play. As he worked with the others, Bill could sense the response that every performer longs for. It was gratifying in a way, but for the first time it didn't seem important. Between lines he was thinking, When you stop enjoying what you're doing, giving it up is no great sacrifice. There would be many nights in future months when Bill would feel very sorry for himself and wonder why he'd given up the only work he felt fitted for, but tonight God allowed him to trust and to prepare for obedience.

The next day, Bill begged to be let free from his contract. He was relieved and surprised when they let him go without any fuss or hard words. Somehow it got through to them that leaving was an absolute necessity. He had no plans for the future—just the conviction that he must make a new start in life.

On returning to New York, Bill became involved with the Christian Arts Fellowship. Jerome Hines, the Metropolitan Opera star, was president. The members were from all areas of show business and the entertainment field: models, singers, actors, dancers, radio and television people. They were the converted people coming out of the Billy Graham Crusade. Some, like Jerome Hines, were already Christians. Lane Adams, a former nightclub singer and entertainer who was studying for the ministry, was brought to New York to work with the new Christians. Maretta Campbell was his executive secretary. Here Bill was thrilled to meet Christian people like Jeanette Clift, Jim Stevenson, and Ron Edmonds from the Billy Graham office. All these people urged him in a kindly way to continue reading his Bible. Bill did this and to his delight discovered that his facility as a "quick study" was a tremendous help in memorizing Bible verses. These days were beautiful to him.

Then there was the matter of earning a living. Bill was still living in his luxurious apartment, but every day he realized more clearly that he must make a radical break with the old life. Almost paradoxically, the only thing he was trained for was the theater, so he continued to make the rounds of the theaters.

Bill was already a church member. Not that it had meant anything to him in the beginning. It wasn't even his idea. While he was teaching dancing at Arthur Murray's, his mother had pressured the pastor at Waxahachie to transfer his letter to New York. More to shut her up than anything else, Bill told them to send the letter to Calvary Baptist Church on Fifty-Seventh Street. The deacons were puzzled by his occupation and equally puzzled when he gave correct answers to all their questions. Dr. Wimbish, who was pastor at the time, may have responded to an urgent plea to keep him associated with a Christian environment. So he was a member; that was about all.

Now that Bill was born again, Calvary Baptist Church became a thrilling place for him. The Reverend Richard Hamilton, interim pastor, and his wife, Ethel, became very close to Bill and contributed much to his early days as a Christian by their wise counsel.

God was speaking to Bill these days—was teaching that he must walk with Him by faith. The first steps were truly frightening ones, for to take them honestly and wholeheartedly, he would need to leave his promising career in the New York theatrical world. Acting was Bill's job security; he was not trained for anything else—except teaching ladies to dance. The second thing Bill knew that he must give up was his comfortable cushion of financial security: his sponsor, Katherine Miles. This lady had helped him through the years and had spent thousands of dollars on his career. Bill knew that somehow he had to end this association and trust in the Lord completely for his future.

During these days, Satan tempted him with the idea that if he could only lead her to Christ, it would be legitimate to remain in her will and to continue to receive her abundant gifts of money. God wouldn't have any part of that, but Bill tried. He took her to Calvary Baptist Church. Then, before it ended, he took her to Billy Graham's crusade. Once he said to her, "Don't you want to go with me to the front?"

She agreed. She went with him to the front. Afterward she said to him, "Nothing happened. What was I supposed to feel? I felt absolutely nothing."

She criticized him for talking so much about Jesus Christ.

"He's very important to me."

"You don't seem to think about anything else now. It's very boring."

One Wednesday night, he took her to a Bible-study prayer meeting. He'd bought her a beautifully bound Bible that day as a gift. Now he watched her fiddling with her diamonds, totally disinterested in the things of God. Realization came to him like a strong electric shock that somehow he must say good-bye to her, not tomorrow, but tonight.

That same day she had said to him, "All your woolen clothes that were stored with my furs at Sak's Fifth Avenue have been delivered to my home. You'd better come and pick them up and take them to your apartment." Included among these were his cashmere overcoat and all the very expensive suits she had showered on him or given him bundles of money to buy. As they went to her home for his winter clothing, Bill realized that this was the time to make known his decision. It meant chopping his earthly security right out from under him. Bill felt sick with fear and anxiety, yet he knew that this was what he must do.

For nearly three hours they sat and talked. Bill began by telling her how God was guiding his life. All the time he was crying silently to the Lord, *You must help me, Lord, my knees are knocking and my will is jelly.*

He went to the bathroom and fell on his knees. He'd prayed about this many times before. He'd tried to make a bargain with God: Find me a job and I'll quit the theater. It seemed now that God didn't want to negotiate; He wanted obedience. Bill pleaded in tears, "Oh, Lord, I don't have the strength to tell her. I'm severing a whole way of life—giving up so much—and I'm scared!" Weeping, he felt so sorry for himself, and yet he was trying to put his trust where it belonged.

Then Bill went out and said to Katherine, "There's never been anybody so kind to me in all my life. Believe me, no human being has ever done so much for me.

. . . But I belong to God now and I must walk with Him by faith. I can't be dependent on anybody else. It's not fair to you; it's not fair to me—and I know it's not what God wants."

Katherine said, "Your rent's due." She picked up her purse and took out another of those rolls of money. "Here," she said. She was challenging him.

"No, Katherine. No, thank you. I don't want any money."

"Well then, I'll see you on Wednesday."

"No. I've got to go now." He managed to get his arms around the plastic bags holding his winter suits and coats, then started for the door.

"I *will* see you on Wednesday, Bill."

He paused at the door. "What I'm trying to say is that I'm not going to see you again."

She fell against the wall, holding to herself as if she had been kicked in the stomach. As she leaned there, trembling all over, a horrible groan came out from the pit of her being.

Then she screamed at him, "My whole life has been you and your career. You can't do this to me—you can't do this to me!"

Bill managed to get the door open. It was ending now, he knew. He was leaving her at last, even if he was still hanging onto the magnificent wardrobe she had given to him. He uttered a weak "God bless you." Then he walked out the door and down the hallway. As he reached its far end, he could still hear Katherine's groans and half-muffled screams.

Bill reached the street and started to call a taxi. Then he realized that he didn't have money for that kind of transportation. Somehow he didn't care and headed for the subway entrance, several blocks away. Weighted down as he was with all the plastic bags filled with his woolen clothing, he felt a buoyancy in his steps. He was very sorry for Katherine and ashamed of the way he had let her pay his first-class passage to Broadway. That was all over now. He was returning to his apartment with no job and one dollar in his pocket. But he had dared to trust the living God—and God had set him free.

6

The next morning Bill went job hunting, dressed in one of his two-hundred-dollar suits with the subway change from his last dollar in his pocket. At the suggestion of Maretta Campbell, from the Billy Graham office, he searched out Loizeaux Brothers, the Christian booksellers and publishers. Strongly identified as Bill was with the glitter of show business, the dingy brownstone building on a trash-littered Eastside street in the garment district came as a shock.

Mr. Loizeaux, a tall and distinguished gray-haired gentleman with a dignified, yet kindly, manner, offered Bill a clerk's job in the retail section of the store. The pay was fifty dollars a week. It was difficult to believe this was actually God's will for his life. Bill wore out shoe leather searching for something else but without success. Then hungry, frightened and desperate for work of any kind, he accepted Mr. Loizeaux's offer.

This was a difficult time of adjustment for Bill. Loizeaux Brothers was the perfect place to deglamorize his outlook on life. When he gave way to frustrated anger, one of his fellow workers would just smile and say in a kindly way, "Oh, Bill, please don't be this way. Try to pray when you get so upset. The Lord knows all about your troubles."

He began to meet some outstanding Christians, some like Dr. Donald Grey Barnhouse, at Calvary Baptist Church, and others through the Christian Arts Fellowship. He was invited into Christian homes where he met people like Dr. M. R. DeHaan and his wife and Dr. Frank E. Gaebelein, headmaster of the famous Stony Brook School. He was meeting magnetic and fruitful Christians, many of them known all over the world, yet it was plain to see that their faith in Christ was the most important part of their lives. It was difficult for Bill to reconcile these exciting acquaintances with the drab and stultifying hours he must spend working at Loizeaux Brothers.

Bill tended to elevate any prominent Christian above the level of mere mortals, not yet realizing that only the Lord God should be revered. Thus he met and was taken in by some Christian frauds until he learned that not everybody who spoke with a Christian vocabulary was genuine.

Experiences like this were unsettling. He became very restless and wondered if he had made a terrible mistake in leaving the theater. Being tempted more than once to return to show business, he went to see a number of shows. Some of these were hits, but when the final curtain dropped, he felt a deepening sense of depression. The magic was gone; the glamour and glitter didn't thrill him anymore. But then, neither did Loizeaux Brothers. A number of times, Bill got out of fellowship with the Lord, only to realize that he could never go back to the old life. Bill Roberts was indeed a new creature, and, although attending church regularly now, he was suffering from growing pains.

One Sunday, moving up the church aisle before evening service Bill spotted a beautiful girl sitting all alone. That night he blocked her exit long enough to look into her face. Under light brown hair were eyes of the deepest blue that caught his for a fleeting instant and then were directed demurely downward. Bill nearly stopped breathing as he told himself with awe, This is the loveliest girl I've seen in my whole life. Following as closely behind her as he dared, he caught her first name as she was greeted by mortals fortunate enough to know her. It was Barbara. He went home repeating the name to himself, Barbara, Barbara. What a beautiful name! What a beautiful girl, so young and fresh that she didn't need any makeup. Upon reflection, he decided that her dress had been rather plain. She didn't need special clothes to look magnificent. No, that wasn't the word for her. Her beauty shone like stars on a crystal-clear night. Oh, well, he'd never see her again. She was visiting somebody. Unattached girls like that were too precious to be found in New York City. But he went to sleep gazing into his recollection of those bluest of eyes.

One night, the pastor's wife, Mrs. Ethel Hamilton, said, "Bill, I'm burdened that you meet a certain girl."

When a man is pushing thirty and still unattached, all the dear ladies are trying to match him up with somebody. Without much enthusiasm, trying to be polite, Bill said, "Now who is it, Mrs. Hamilton?"

"Oh, dear me. I can't think of her name, but stand here

with me and I'll point her out as she comes through the door." They came through the door, plain Janes and washed-out blondes and all the rest of the unexciting girls, probably longing for a little male attention. Bill was thinking about some polite excuse to get lost when Mrs. Hamilton said, "There she is!"

Then Barbara came through the door. Bill nearly hugged Mrs. Hamilton, who seemed astonished at his excitement as he whispered, "That's the girl I've been praying about! I'm just dying to meet her!"

Moments later, he somehow survived his introduction to Barbara Precht, from Napoleon, Ohio, and with joy discovered that she lived and worked in New York City.

The church held a retreat at the Percy Crawford Camp in the Pocono Mountains of Pennsylvania. Bill went, hoping that Barbara would be there. She had never come to any but the regular church services and he'd had no chance to really get to know her. One hundred and twenty-five of them went up in individual cars, but Bill didn't see Barbara anywhere.

At seven o'clock the next morning, Bill opened his cabin door. Out under a tree clothed in autumn's golden leaves and standing beside the bluest of lakes stood Barbara. Joy flooded his soul; he knew he had all weekend to get to know her. Only six other guys had the same idea. This became obvious when they all tried to sit at her table. At one informal gathering in the lounge, there were sofas scattered all about. Barbara had hardly seated herself when there was a rush to sit beside her. Bill got there first and began to sit down. Somebody paused to speak to him and he remained standing for a couple of seconds, then sat down on the lap of another young fellow. The entire weekend went the same way, but he did manage to get a date with her for the following Monday.

They were to have dinner together and then go to hear Dr. Donald Barnhouse in one of his Monday night Bible studies. They walked down Fifth Avenue together, her hand gently holding the crook of his arm, and it came upon him with a rush of feeling he'd never experienced before that he was in love with Barbara. How blessed to be alone with her at last!

Somebody walked up behind them and tapped Bill on the shoulder. Startled, he turned to find one of the city's poor derelicts in shabby clothing, asking them for money. Barbara turned around and in her sweet way she touched him on his dirty sleeve as she said, "Do you know that Jesus loves you very much and died for you? Why don't you come to eat with us now?" Her sweetness and simple sincerity affected Bill deeply. He knew at the time that he wouldn't have suggested such a thing himself, but when he heard her say that, he fell more deeply in love with her. They ate a simple meal together. Under the wreckage, Bill could see that the man had once had self-respect, an education, and no doubt a good job. But as Barbara sat with the two of them she conveyed the impression that they were all equal in God's sight and blessed by His great love.

They had a beautiful date that night. After the Bible study, they went out into the night together. After walk-

ing and talking for some time they wanted to pray together and looked for a church that was open, but
couldn't find one. They walked up to Tudor City. There,
beside an iron-rail fence and looking down over the U. N.
Building with the wind in their faces, they prayed a simple prayer.

They walked back to the automat to have tea together.
As they sat there, Bill asked, "Barbara, do you think that
two people who are meant for each other by God will
know it?"

She said, "Well, I guess so." Bill didn't know it, but she
was less than thrilled by his remark. She'd learned just
that evening that Bill was ten years older than her mere
nineteen. So she was thinking sadly, He can't possibly be
talking about us. There's no chance he'll ever be serious
about me.

He called her on the phone every night. He thought
about her all the time. He began to see her every day—
at least for a little bit. And she told him about herself.

Barbara's parents were of German stock and she grew
up in a community that was almost totally Lutheran. Her
grandfather had been a Lutheran pastor and she attended
a parochial school, where she learned hundreds of Bible
verses. A shy girl, she had only a few dates in high school
and these had been chaperoned by one of her four brothers. She had no sisters, and was so quiet that nobody
guessed what she dreamed about.

Her dream was to leave that little Ohio town and to go
to New York City. She thought it would be better to be

dead than to waste her life in Napoleon, Ohio, population, 6,739.

Barbara's first job in New York was a routine one for an advertising agency. Here she met people who saw in her real modeling potential. A photographer began to use her as a model. She went to the Barbizon School of Models. They taught her how to apply makeup, how to dress, how to pose. After she began seeking modeling jobs, attractive young men she was meeting began asking her for dates. These experiences brought poise and a measure of self-assurance, but she never lost the sweet modesty and shy quality of trustfulness which were such attractive facets of her personality.

As the gap widened between her new life and the life she had known at home, she found it harder to communicate with her family. Eventually she stopped writing home. She found modeling interesting. Still, it all fell short of her girlhood dreams. Some vital element was missing.

On July 5, 1957, Barbara decided to attend the Billy Graham Crusade in Madison Square Garden. She went to that great auditorium where there had been no garden for many years. She passed inside under the brightly lighted sign which read:

MADISON SQUARE GARDEN
NIGHTLY AT 7:30 P.M.
BILLY GRAHAM
NEW YORK CRUSADE
AIR-CONDITIONED
ALL SEATS FREE

Barbara listened intently during the service. Like so many others, she knew about Jesus Christ with her head, yet though she had clung to her confirmation Bible for security, she had never committed her life to Him. Sitting there, listening to Mr. Graham, it struck her forcibly that the only real security any person can have is through Jesus Christ, the Son of the living God. She wanted to know Him personally. Her extremely sensitive nature gave her a strong sense of personal guilt, and she learned with a tremendous sense of relief that she could drop the whole burden at Christ's feet and be His own child. She'd never been in a service where people went to the front, acknowledging Christ as Saviour and Lord. But this night she was drawn so strongly to Him that she forgot about what others might think and went eagerly down the aisle.

After this, Barbara attended Bible-study classes across the Hudson in New Jersey. She met Christian friends. She was thrilled by her new life as a Christian and no longer cared to be a model. She soon went to work for Shell Oil Company. Some people she met at this time in her life encouraged her to take off all her makeup and to dress plainly and conservatively. Given her remarkable beauty, her fresh young face was enough to attract an army, though Barbara would never have believed this herself.

Then she began attending Calvary Baptist Church and after a few weeks met Bill Roberts, at that time president of one of the young professional groups which met there.

Bill felt his romance with Barbara was the most beautiful experience of his life up to that time. On crisp nights they walked down the streets, hand in hand. They laughed and ran and shared the magic moments of simple little meals together. They went together to Christian Arts Fellowship, began to attend Bible studies following a meal, inviting people they wanted to reach for the Lord. Then, while dating Barbara, Bill felt that perhaps he was called into the ministry. He wanted to serve God. Bill and Barbara agreed together that to serve the King of kings and the Lord of lords, the Creator of the universe and the God of their salvation—was the greatest privilege in all the world.

This must have been a matter of concern for the devil, who tempted Bill and won the next round. One day in November at Loizeaux Brothers, Bill was so completely defeated in his Christian life that in a spectacular fit of temper, he ran out of the place and never went back again.

Now he was out of work again and needed a job badly. After what he had done, he could never ask Mr. Loizeaux for a recommendation. A defeated Christian, Bill sat in Central Park with his little New Testament in his pocket. The mist turned to a cold rain. Bill moved to a seat under a tree with heavy foliage and returned to his dark thoughts. He was at the end of himself and didn't know which way to turn. He'd given God his career and his dating girls. Now he wondered what God could do with a Bill Roberts. What could He do with an ex-dancer, ex-actor, whose life had been wild and undisciplined. He'd lived at night so long that it was hard to get up in the morning. He felt so ineffectual, weak and miserable.

Then he remembered someone had said that when you

reach the end of yourself, that's where God can really take
over your life. He pulled out the little New Testament,
and shielding the pages carefully from the rain, read the
fourth chapter of Hebrews very carefully. Truths were
revealed there which he had not noticed before. "But the
word preached did not profit them, not being mixed with
faith in them that heard it" (verse 2). The next truth that
took hold of him was the matter of entering into God's
rest through belief. He thought about that. Then he ab-
sorbed verse twelve. God knew all about Bill Roberts,
sitting there on a dripping park bench, ready to give up.
He felt convicted and yet at the same time wonderfully
assured. Then his eyes hovered over the last verse: "Let
us therefore come boldly to the throne of grace, that we
may obtain mercy, and find grace to help in time of
need."

Sighing with relief, Bill returned the testament to his
pocket. Here was his answer for today. He had been
tiptoeing up to receive God's divine love and protection.
With a feeling of new freedom and boldness, he said
aloud, "Oh, God, here's my life. Do with it what you will;
I give you all of me." Feeling like a new man, Bill strode
out of Central Park and caught a bus.

He was walking into Sak's Fifth Avenue to apply for a
Christmas job when he met an old buddy from show busi-
ness days. "I haven't seen you for months!" the fellow said.
"Come, let's have coffee."

While sitting in Schrafft's, just around the corner, Bill
told this young man what had happened to him. These
days he told everybody what Christ had done in his life.

Bill was used to faint smiles or painful silences from old friends. This fellow reacted in violent blasphemy. Jesus and his disciples were homosexuals. . . . Filth poured out in a compulsive rage.

Bill was stunned. He had never heard such filth come out of a person's mouth. "You can't talk like that about Him! Jesus is my Saviour. I love Him; He's changed my life."

The actor looked at Bill with hatred and snarled, "Well, if you love Him so much, why don't you become a preacher?" He gulped the last of his coffee, slammed down his cup and rose to leave.

Bill began to walk out with him but the man walked faster to get away. Bill called out his name and said, "I'm going to pray for you."

The actor threw back his head and screamed, "Don't you bother to pray for me!"

All over the place, people were staring. Bill hardly noticed. He'd forgotten about the Christmas job and went out and walked on and on in the rain. He felt numb, almost stunned from what that fellow had said—such unspeakable filth about the One he'd come to know and love so much. He walked over to Rockefeller Center. The rain had stopped; the air was crisp and cold. He stopped and looked down at the skaters circling below. Without conscious effort on his part, it seemed that his inner being was whirling like a piece of smooth-working machinery, connecting and sorting out bits and pieces from the last few months' experiences.

Then the significance of it all hit him; it was hammered

into his consciousness, and even welded there by the
shock of the filthy words thrown at him by a lost soul from
the world he had left. Bill shook his head while the skaters
whirled below. Yes, there was no doubt about it; *he was
called into the ministry!* That dirty mouth had just
brought out in the open something precious that had
been locked in with his self-doubts and uncertainties as to
his work and any possible future with Barbara. It was true,
they had talked about his serving the Lord, but he realized now that this had just been a beautiful abstraction
without legs to carry it into action and reality. What was
that verse? "Therefore come boldly . . . ." That was it. He
had nothing to fear. With God's grace he would really do
it. It was not man calling him. It was not feeling a sense
of duty to serve God. It was God calling him through
every fiber of his being. The Saviour was calling him into
His ministry. He was conscious of the date; it was November 13, 1958. Immediately he got a severe headache from
the shock and awesomeness of the call of God, but he was
happy and filled with a sense of wonderful peace.

Bill kept on walking until he reached Calvary Baptist
Church and asked the secretary if Reverend Hamilton
was in. He was, and Bill told him of his call into the ministry. The pastor didn't seem surprised.

"I've watched God doing things in your life. I felt certain He was about to call you."

Bill called his mother in Waxahachie. She said, "Bill.
Oh, Bill! You know, when you were around eighteen,
before you ever became a Christian, I woke up one night,
feeling very strongly, as if from God, *My son will be called*

to preach some day!"

Most of the people he told about it said something like, "Oh, we're not surprised." And Bill thought to himself, That's funny, it seems like everybody knew but me.

7

Members of the Christian Arts Fellowship were over-joyed at Bill's decision. He'd be one of the first in the group to be called into full-time Christian service. He didn't know what phase of the work God wanted him to enter. He felt sure that would be made clear in due time.

When he told Barbara his news, she was quietly pleased. He wondered a bit about that, not realizing that she had jumped ahead of his euphoria to the practical hurdles facing him.

It was time to wind up his affairs in New York and to complete the semester lacking for his degree at the University of Texas. After that, seminary. Leaving his beloved New York was one thing; the city would always be there waiting for his return. Barbara was another matter. He didn't feel that his call included giving her up!

Watching the skaters at Rockefeller Center with Barbara beside him, he blurted, "Barbara, I love you. You know I have to leave New York in a few days. Will you marry me?"

She said, "Bill, I love you too, but not with all my heart. I still don't know God's will for my life and I can't say yes."

He liked her answer. Somehow, God had shown him

that Barbara was the right one for him—He just hadn't shown her yet. Bill was willing to help God with this problem in any way possible.

A few days later, in a taxi together, he asked her again and she quietly answered, "Yes."

Bill looked up. It was at Fifty-Fifth and Madison that she'd said yes. For him, forever after, Fifty-Fifth and Madison was a beautiful spot. He was quite verbal about her saying yes. He told a number of people and then noticed Barbara getting very quiet and frightened-looking. Afterwards, she told him that although she had been praying about her decision, her answer had "slipped out" without her really intending it. She stayed awake most of that night, praying and thinking. Then peace flooded her heart and from then on she never doubted that Bill was God's choice—the man she should marry.

The next business at hand for Bill was closing the apartment he had regarded with so much affection as his home.

Two days later, he bought a Greyhound bus ticket back to Texas. He said good-bye to the lovely girl who had promised to become his wife. Their understanding was that they'd be married as soon as he got his degree. One semester to go. What an incentive! The Mission Board of Calvary Baptist promised a little money for tuition and books. This was a tremendous help as he had very little saved up and left New York pretty much as he had arrived seven years earlier: broke and on a bus.

Waxahachie was directly on the road to Austin. Bill stopped there for a visit with his mother and the feeble little grandmother who still lived on. They were alone in the old home, as Bill's younger brother was now married. His mother was filled with joy that her prayers had been answered and looked forward with enthusiasm to her son's future in the ministry. It was strange, how differently he felt about the many Christian friends of the family. Their lives no longer seemed dull and uninteresting. It came as a shock for him to realize that the big change had taken place, not with them, but within himself.

Soon Bill went on to Austin and enrolled for his final semester. It was now the spring of 1959 and he had matriculated here in the autumn of 1948, over ten years earlier. Immediately he was caught up in a wonderful fellowship of Christians. He had introductions from New York friends to Austin's Evangelical Free Church. On campus he soon met young Christian students and the staff of Campus Crusade. The latter became excited when they learned of Bill's background in drama. There were twenty-three thousand students at the University of Texas and while successful elsewhere, the Campus Crusade people had not been able to breach what seemed like fortified walls around the drama department.

There was a handsome young man in Bill's drama class. He was perfect material for romantic leads, except for the handicap of a long Texas drawl. He came to Bill and said, "You're a Texan and you've lost your accent. Will you help me with my speech problem?"

"Sure, John. You just come over any time and we'll work on your Texas vowels."

The next day, John arrived carrying a great stack of

books. They began to work on his diction, reading a number of scenes, speeches and poems. Then Bill, who'd been wondering how to witness to the fellow, said, "John, do you know that there's a book that's quite difficult to read audibly to do justice to the beautiful cadence and the majesty of the wording?"

"What book is tha-at, Bill?"

"Why, the Bible." Bill turned to the third chapter of John's gospel and had him read it aloud. While John read this chapter, his voice dropped quieter and quieter as the message of God's Word began to speak to his heart. Out of it came a chance to witness to him and explain what this meant. In a little while, John bowed his head and in his Texas drawl, asked Jesus Christ to forgive his sins and to come into his life. Before he had finished his short prayer, Dick Ballew, of Campus Crusade, knocked on the door and met a new brother in Christ.

They began to meet every day, to read the Bible while they worked on John's accent. Out of this meeting, others in the drama department became interested in Bible study and joined the group. One young man had once been active in Young Life and now he rededicated his life to the Lord. Another, who had claimed to be an atheist at a Campus Crusade retreat, received Christ and then his buddy became interested and found the Lord. This chain reaction began to move and to change a considerable part of the drama department.

The group from the drama department began to meet regularly for Bible study. One day when Bill stopped at the desk in the Student Union to check out a room, the lady there said, "I'm sorry, I can't check out a room to you. It's been reported that you're preaching in the Student Union and the dean wants to see you."

Bill told the kids they'd been refused a room. It didn't really seem important; they sat on the lawn and read the Bible together. Then Bill went to see the dean who said, "It's been reported that you are preaching and teaching the Bible in Student Union."

Bill said, "Well, really I'm not. I'm no preacher. We're just reading the Bible."

The dean asked, "Do you have a faculty sponsor?"

"No, sir. It's not a club."

"But you'll have to get a faculty sponsor."

"Well, sir, it's all right. We don't really need a room. We sat on the lawn today."

"On campus?"

"Yes, sir. Is that bad?"

"Bill, I'm trying to tell you that you can't do that sort of thing on campus. What could keep you from the next thing—preaching on the Student Union steps?"

Bill smiled. "Well, I guess nothing."

"Well, you'll have to get off the campus to do that sort of thing."

Word spread through the drama department that a room had been refused for Bible study. The next day, people came from all directions—students who had never attended before, some of them carrying big, family-type Bibles. They left campus in a group and went to sit on the lawn by the church. The weekly Bible study became a tremendous success. This was before the days of campus protests. It was just a natural reaction to having Bible study prohibited on campus. The action had been taken to prevent the study, but God turned it into a help.

One day, one of Bill's profs did a caricature of him, trying to humiliate him before the group. The prof did a beautiful picture with pleading gestures as he begged in unctuous tones, *"Will you come to my Bible study?"* He meant to mock the whole business, but he was actually advertising the Bible study and as a result, even more attended. Bill was learning some new truths about Romans 8:28.

Day and night, Bill's thoughts went back over the miles to Barbara in New York. He'd met her in October and left early in January. They'd been together less than three months and had been separated four and a half months now. Every day he looked for the mailman and cherished every word of every letter she wrote him. He could hardly wait until he had completed work for his degree, as she had promised to marry him then.

Barbara left New York City on a cold, rainy night, and a very trying three months began upon her arrival home in Napoleon. Toward the end of that time it seemed almost a dream that she had ever been in New York or that she was to marry Bill. By this time, Bill was deeply involved in Campus Crusade activities at Austin and in completing studies for his degree. His letters, sweet and loving as they were, contained such enthusiastic reports that Barbara fell victim to self-doubts. Her sense of confidence suffered as she compared what she considered her modest gifts with Bill's confident air, his education, experience and important friends.

To add to Barbara's anxieties, whenever Bill phoned her from Texas, he seemed less than satisfied with her end of the conversations. Barbara didn't know how to explain to him that as her folks didn't have a phone at the time, she had given him the neighbor's number to call. The result was that as they talked, she was surrounded by a fascinated audience of relatives, friends and neighbors, all eager to hear something romantic. As Bill pleaded for affectionate responses from Barbara, he had no idea that his bashful bride-to-be was playing to a full house.

Meanwhile, down in Austin, Bill thought that Barbara would never come if they didn't set a definite date. This spurred him into making a definite date with Barbara— which of course was what she had been anxiously waiting for. Near the end of the semester and the completion of his degree, he phoned Barbara to come down to Texas right away. The few weeks remaining before their wedding, she could stay with his mother in Waxahachie. So Barbara packed her bags and all the accumulation of wedding gifts and boarded a bus in Napoleon.

Although Bill's mother was expecting her, Barbara had failed to send on her time of arrival in Waxahachie. She herself had no idea of such details—just bought the ticket, checked her baggage and climbed on board.

They arrived in Waxahachie at two o'clock the next morning. The town had no bus station. There were no taxis. Barbara felt panic closing in as she stepped down into the dark and deserted street. The bus driver was not one to desert her alone in a strange town with the side-walks rolled up. He got hold of a police officer, who volunteered to deliver Barbara in his patrol car.

During the next few days word spread through Waxahachie that a very young, very pretty girl had arrived from up north to marry Bill Roberts and nobody met her. They said Bill was still in Austin, 200 miles away! That gave a few tongues a chance to wag. When some of this got back to Barbara, she was mortified, but Bill's mother comforted her with a cheerful, "Never mind them folks, honey. Everybody in Waxahachie knows Bill Roberts don't plan ahead."

8

Bill was finally graduated from the University of Texas. He came off the Austin bus at Waxahachie, rushing up the steps to his mother's porch, pushing through the crowd of well-wishers and the curious, to hold Barbara in his arms. She was the girl God had given him and they were to be married at last!

They had planned a very simple wedding. Barbara's parents had three boys still in school and as they were unable to come so far, had sent their gifts. Bill and Barbara knew that the seminary days ahead would be lean and hungry. Then Bill's sister-in-law, Janet—lonely because her husband was on Army duty in Germany—begged them to let her plan a garden wedding. She had her beautiful wedding gown fitted for Barbara, who made a truly lovely bride. Janet arranged an archway in the garden, with candlelabra, potted plants and a white pathway. On June 13, 1959, Barbara and Bill were married under the Texas stars.

After the wedding, the minister called Bill aside and said, "I know you don't have lots of money. Why don't you folks go in to Dallas for a couple of days and then you come back and go with me to speak at a conference in Livingston."

Bill thought, Not on my honeymoon! and began to beg off, but the minister talked him into it.

They shared two happy days in a lovely hotel. Then they joined the Reverend and Mrs. L. H. Raney for the conference in Livingston, a small county seat. After the two-hundred-mile drive, during which the newlyweds were unable to exchange a word in private, the Raneys put them up in an adjoining motel room. Here, listening to the hearty conversations of the Raneys coming through the thin partition, they were at least able to communicate in whispers. By this time, Bill doubted that this "honeymoon" expedition could possibly be in the perfect will of God, which they had prayed for so earnestly in Dallas. "We should have stayed alone!" he muttered to Barbara, but they tried to laugh it off as he went out to do his little speaking and dramatic reading chores.

Back in Waxahachie, they learned a bit more about life the hard way. Instead of planning ahead, spreading their money thin and renting some little apartment, they lived from day to day until their money was nearly gone, then moved into a small upstairs room in Bill's mother's home. Relatives came and went in an easygoing manner, raising their eyebrows knowingly and making their newlywed jokes around a couple who should have been alone while making their adjustments.

Bill began to notice how quiet and shy Barbara was. When she was subjected to a barrage of curious questions, her brief answers often faded into silence. Then the more talkative Bill, at home in his Texas, all too often took over the answering for her. This only pressed Barbara more firmly into her shell. If there was a chance to slip away and be alone, she would leave the group. Often he found her out among the flowers in somebody's garden. Another time, after a considerable search, he found her walking in the woods alone. While he was falling in love with her and urging her to marry him, Bill had not noticed how quietly introverted Barbara was—that she was a meditator, not a talker, and that her friends loved her just as she was. Well, he loved her more than anyone on earth, but he'd have to straighten her out.

He didn't have much success straightening her out. They were driving to Fort Worth to visit Bill's aunt and it seemed like the right time to explain his point of view, so he did. Barbara just sat in the car, tearing at her handkerchief. She didn't answer him—not one word. As soon as they arrived at the aunt's house, Bill said to Barbara, "Let's take a walk. I've got something to say to you."

She didn't take his arm, so he grabbed hers and got her started along in a reluctant walk as he said, almost in her ear, "Barbara, I want to tell you something. God has called me into the ministry and therefore you are called into the ministry. And you may be shy and quiet and introverted. But let's call it what it really is, it's sin. You're self-centered and what's more, you're foolish to be so quiet. You *must* commit this to God. How can we go into the ministry if you're not going to be friendly and cordial to people?"

Tears were running down Barbara's cheeks. Bill was thinking, This is pretty cruel, but somebody has to tell her. He said, "You're living in a dreamworld. You've never faced reality before. I understand, because that's the kind of world I lived in—make-believe."

Barbara jerked away from him. Between sobs, her words leaped out at him with a courage that startled him. "Who's living in a dreamworld, Bill Roberts? You've just exchanged the stage for a dream pulpit and now you think you're Billy Graham or Dr. Criswell—or somebody! I'm your wife, and you say you love me. Well, are you being cordial and friendly to me?"

"But Barbara. . . ."

"But nothing! That's enough for today, Mr. Roberts. Thank you very much!" Sobbing, she whirled around and ran off a few steps, then continued walking away from him down the country lane.

Bill was steaming. He wasn't about to capitulate, and stalked back to his aunt's house. Then as soon as he got there and Barbara was out of sight, he began to worry for her physical safety. All alone down a country lane—no telling who she might meet. Why, Barbara could be in terrible danger. He must go find her.

Barbara had not gone far. He found her leaning over a fence, watching some cows grazing. He came up and put his arm around her. "I love you, Barbara. . . . And there was some truth in what you said. I guess we don't have to be the same to love each other and to serve the Lord." Barbara was crying again as her arm went around her husband's neck, but these were happy tears.

Other problems arose between them, but they managed to survive each in turn. Bill began to realize that he had been trying to make Barbara over into something she wasn't. Though they were very much in love and though they communicated beautifully about Jesus, they were realizing that they really knew so very little about each other. Each new lesson came as a minor or major shock. And then their life together went on a little better. They were experiencing what a mariner would call a successful shakedown cruise. The love of Christ and the genuine love that God had given each for the other kept them safe from the rocks and shoals of matrimony while they became adjusted, one to another.

9

Bill was accepted at Dallas Theological Seminary. With his degree in drama and his career on the New York stage behind him, he entered as a somewhat less-than-confident student. He and Barbara settled temporarily in a run-down apartment with a leaky roof. They shared the bathroom with a couple in the next apartment who fought vehemently at all hours of the day and night. In this delightful environment, they continued their marriage adjustments while Barbara worked at Hartford Insurance Company and Bill struggled with his assigned studies.

Barbara, one of this world's most uncertain navigators, got lost trying to get home from her first day at the office. Confused as to direction and distance, she got off the bus many blocks too soon. Bill paced the floor, then paced the streets, seeking his lost bride. At last he sighted a weary girl going down another street in the wrong direction. He hollered, "Barbara!" and ran after her.

As they hugged each other, she said tremulously, "Oh, Bill, I was so lost! I'd forgotten our address and I didn't know what I was going to do."

Barbara was not the only one who felt bewildered. Matriculation at Dallas Theological Seminary was a frighten-

ing experience. At that point, Bill had hardly read his
Bible through. His counselor, Dr. Evans, said, "Oh, Bill,
for anybody to get married and then come straight to
seminary—especially from your background. You need
prayer!"

Greek was really Greek to Bill! In his first testimony as
a new man at Dallas, he said, "Greek is my first class in the
morning, but let me tell you gentlemen, it's 'Greek' all
day long! I don't understand the meanings of these words
you're using. I can't spell them either and I'm blundering
in the dark all day." They laughed, but he was just being
truthful.

Barbara and Bill soon reached the point when they felt
that they could never last the winter in their shabby
apartment—what with the leaks and the noise. Then they
found an apartment in a government housing project in
West Dallas. The section they moved into was near an
area called Convicts' Row because it was populated for
the most part by the "widows" of prisoners and their
children. A number of seminary students were living
among them. It was first necessary to qualify as "low in-
come," which was no problem to Bill and Barbara. Some
people were horrified at the thought of these theological
students living in what was considered a dangerous place,
even in daytime. Yet it proved to be a fruitful combina-
tion. Within walking distance were thousands of spiritu-
ally deprived children, the majority black, who responded gladly to Good News clubs, as these were
organized.

Actually, these little apartments near Convicts' Row

were attractive and cozy with two bedrooms above a kitchen and living room. Bill and Barbara soon established friendships there with other seminary student couples. Harold and Roma Brown had been married the same day as Bill and Barbara. Roma, having previous experience with Good News clubs, decided to start one in her apartment. Barbara gladly volunteered to help her. After the first few meetings, they packed that little apartment with children, some of them dirty-faced and barefoot. The two girls showed such a sweet spirit that some of these little boys and girls came to love them and then through them, to know and love Jesus Christ as their Saviour.

The first to accept Christ was a beautiful, angelic-looking blonde girl who stood out like a jewel among the more nondescript children. Her parents lived near enough for Bill and Barbara to hear her mother screaming while being beaten by her drunken father. A few years later, Bill was speaking at a family-type banquet in Dallas. In walked the mother of this little girl, now fresh faced, happy and attractive. Then in came the father with all of their children. As they took their seats together, Bill mentioned to someone that he'd known them. "Oh, yes. After that one little girl became a Christian, she was baptized. And after that, one by one, every one of her brothers and sisters and then the mother and father came to know the Saviour." This was just one incident out of many changed lives from this one Good News club.

Seminary continued to be difficult for Bill. The discipline of study was so different from that of the theater. Monday was his day off and when Barbara went to work,

Bill often sat with the shades down and the lights off, almost in a state of shock. Though his head throbbed and his brain seemed overpowered as he tried to absorb the outpourings of his professors and the knowledge dug from books, especially from the Book of books, he was learning a great deal. God was doing a work in him.

Then his show-business experience began to serve in a completely new dimension. He was invited to speak in churches like Scofield Memorial, and at various meetings and banquets. Dallas Seminary asked his help in putting on their Christmas program. He did so and also gave them his "Texas Shakespeare." He would give readings from *Macbeth,* first as he had done them on the stage, and then in an exaggerated Texas drawl that invariably would bring down the house. Bill felt humbly grateful for what he came to think of as these "loaves and fishes" of his life, which became a sort of trademark of his ministry and opened many areas of witness.

While Bill was getting a broad foundation for future ministry, he also began to see the impact of drama in the Christian field. As God began to guide him in this direction, he began to write little two-character plays that could be performed in simple situations. As he looked back on them later, they certainly were not masterpieces, yet they could be very effective. Most were contemporary-type situations that had as their solutions words from the gospels showing the way of salvation.

He was also meeting future leaders in the Christian world—people like Gordon Mohr, president of their class, and his wife, Beverly, Thayer and Thelia Nightingale,

John Hartog and Charles Swindoll.

One day, John Hartog, who had written a number of tracts, said, "Bill, I'd like to do a tract on your life." He showed some of his earlier work, not very attractively printed, but with effective messages. Bill agreed.

John incorporated an organization called World For Christ, and a number of the fellows became involved. As a pilot tract, they did one on Bill. The story was written by John and the cover done by Gordon Mohr, an expert in photography and art work. The tract, containing the simple testimony of Bill's life to that point, was attractive and professional-looking. Then, Thayer Nightingale said, "You know, I feel led to send this to Billy Graham and see if his team may be interested in doing a larger story for *Decision* magazine." Eventually this little tract did open the way for Bill's story to be published in *Decision* in March, 1963.

These friends talked together about future plans. Gordon Mohr expected to become a professional photographer and do documentary films on mission fields. He was planning to stay one year only at Dallas Theological Seminary, and after that to take more professional training in photography. Together with John Hartog and some of the others, Gordon thought that they might film perhaps thirteen of the plays Bill had written. With Bill and Barbara acting the star parts, they could be used for Christian television or in the churches. As they talked, Gordon recalled that there was an old studio in Portland, Oregon, that had facilities for making films such as these.

It seemed to Bill that God was guiding wonderfully, so

he began to plan in this direction. When Gordon mentioned that he'd gone to Multnomah School of the Bible there in Portland and that they had an excellent one-year graduate Bible course, Bill felt sure that all would work out well. They could film the plays in three months. Then he could either return to Dallas for the next year in seminary, or he could go to Multnomah. His thinking was a bit vague and he had not actually sat down with pencil and paper to figure how all this was to be financed. At this point in his life, Bill was not noteworthy for planning ahead.

As the seminary year finished, Bill and Barbara had no money to finance the trip to Portland. Bill's brother, Tommy, who was now a car dealer, had gotten a car of sorts for Bill to drive around Dallas. It was a vintage Pontiac, very reliable in that it could be trusted to break down during nearly any trip longer than a few city blocks. When Bill shared his vision of what they would do in Portland, Oregon, his mother could understand this as an adventure of faith. But his brother Tommy, the practical one of the family, couldn't understand it.

He said, "Bill, you're a fool to try this. That old clunker won't get out of Dallas. You can't take it across the country."

Sure enough, the next day the car broke down with a dramatic throwing of pistons, still in Dallas. Then Bill phoned his mother and Tommy, and told them excitedly, "God has provided another way. He always has!" Roma and Harold Brown were going to visit their homes in Oregon and had promised Barbara and Bill a ride to Portland. They were leaving earlier than expected, so Bill phoned his mother again. He said, "Mother, we have to leave right now. Will you have Tommy pack our things and keep them for us?"

So Bill and his faithful Barbara hurriedly packed one bag each and left the apartment to jump into the Browns' car for the West Coast. There were dirty dishes in the sink, clothing here and there—a house in a government project filled with oddments of furniture and a broken-down Pontiac—all to be taken care of.

Bill would look back with regret to the poor witness he had been to his brother and the unnecessary trouble he had caused him by his thoughtless lack of planning. But now, with the Browns, they rushed westward, night and day—all the way to Portland. Bill and Barbara found it a delirious kind of trip, over mountains, across deserts and on into the lush country of western Oregon. The Browns dropped them off in Portland and drove off to visit their families in Eugene and Medford, then back to Dallas. This had been a one-way ride.

At the time of arrival, Bill and Barbara had no apartment and no friends anywhere near. Multnomah had no summer session. Everything concerning the filming of Bill's little plays fell through as the others involved were led into other activities. They were in a strange city, thousands of miles from their former homes with something like fifteen dollars total capital.

When Bill learned that there was no chance whatever to film his plays, he tried to understand the purpose for which he and Barbara found themselves in such a place.

The answer seemed to be that he should take the graduate course at Multnomah School of the Bible. They went
to see Miss Joyce Kehoe, the registrar.

She said, "I don't believe I've received your admission
papers. Did you mail them ahead?"

"Oh—no," he said. "But. . . ."

"Well, where have you come from?"

"From Texas," he said, brightening up. "I know Gordon
Mohr. He recommended that I come here."

Miss Kehoe laughed. "We're glad to have the recommendation, but *you* need a recommendation too, you
know."

They went over the details. He had his degree, plus the
year at Dallas. Other details were tuition, registration fee,
the nonresident student requirement to have a minimum
of $110 left over, transcripts, physical, references.

Bill thanked Miss Kehoe and they left. "No problems at
all, Barbara, except we have no money, no jobs and no
place to stay."

They found an apartment of sorts, on Northeast Glisan
Street, near the school. It was over an old-fashioned
butcher shop, reached by a long, dark staircase and a
dimly-lit hall. The bath fixtures belonged in the Smith-
sonian as an exhibit of antiquity, while the smell of fish,
coming up the radiator, permeated the three dismal
rooms. The retired butcher who owned the apartment
decided that they were honest. He told them they might
move in without payment in advance. "But don't keep me
waiting too long. I ain't rich—can't afford charity."

They thanked their new landlord and carried up their

luggage. The furniture, such as it was, would have to do. They remembered with longing all the useful things left behind in Dallas. Work was hard to find; summer jobs were already filled. They walked the streets and followed every lead, without results. They got down to one dollar. While they talked of what food they should buy with it— a loaf of bread, milk, a bite of hamburger, perhaps—they both felt convicted about the lack of tithing in their lives together. "We've been so lackadaisical about giving back to Him," Bill said. "How can we plead with Him to do all that we ask?" So they went to church and put their last dollar in the collection plate.

They went hungry that Sunday and Satan came to haunt them and to taunt them. *Why didn't you buy food?* They were expecting Barbara's final paycheck from Dallas, but it didn't come. The landlord was expecting his rent. He said, "Well, if you two are serious about working, I'll tell you what I'll do. They've begun to pick beans out in the country. We'll leave early, five in the morning. I'll take you out there."

At five in the morning he was there at the door. He drove them miles out into the country and dropped them off at a bean field. The landlord said, "I'm not coming back for you. They have buses that will bring you back to town."

Bill looked around. In Texas they had tiny little rows of beans that you stooped down to pick. This was Oregon. There were miles of great vines that grew on poles and hung from strings. Their fellow pickers were from the Portland skid road or the slums.

Bill said, "You've got to pick too, Barbara. I'm not going to pick beans by myself." Barbara was willing to pick beans, but she looked very bewildered—and Bill was wondering how to fill the buckets somebody had thrust into their hands. Their names were down on the chart and it was time to get started.

Nearby was a jolly black woman who had begun to work. Bill went up to her and said, "I beg your pardon. Could you tell me what part of the bean to pick? Do you pick not only the bean but the stem? Do you pick the stem off?"

She laughed and said, "Darlin', pick the bean, the stem, the leaves—even put in rocks. Make it weigh heavy!"

That was their short course in bean picking. Soon Barbara and Bill began to laugh too. She picked on one side of a row while he picked on the other. Every now and them they came to a break in the vines and sneaked a kiss. For a while it was a sort of fun day; then it rained until they were wet and muddy. They picked all day long. Between the two of them, they earned only four dollars and twenty cents, but it was cash money for food. By now, they weren't thinking of anything fancy. Bread, meat, and potatoes, that's what they'd get. Dirty and soaking wet, they climbed into the battered old pickers' bus together with the hard-pressed mothers and the poor derelicts who now had money for another bottle. The bus let Bill and Barbara off many blocks from their destination. Embarrassed by their appearance, they trudged toward their butcher-shop apartment. There they feasted upon the simple food that they had bought and agreed that it tasted better than the finest dinner at the Waldorf-Astoria Hotel in New York.

A few days later the food was gone, they still had no work, and were hungry again. They read the Bible a lot and prayed together, asking for guidance, asking to be used. One day they were reading in Exodus 21:6 about the bored-ear servant who gave himself willingly to serve the master he loved. They fell on their knees then and Bill prayed, "Oh, God! Let us be your love slaves!"

It did not occur to them to ask for charity, or to try and go on relief. They were hungry enough to slip down to the garbage can in back of the butcher shop and pick over the refuse. All they found was a box of chicken bones. They took these upstairs, washed them fastidiously, then set them to boil. They'd been married nine or ten months and remembered the honeymoon rice that was still littered around inside their suitcases. They gathered up every grain of this rice, which came to a handful, washed it and put it on to boil with the chicken bones. Then they gnawed all the gristle from the bones, drank the broth and ate the few spoonfuls of rice.

A man knocked at their door. This came as a surprise; the average person would never dream anybody lived above that run-down butcher shop. He said, "I've never come up here before, but I just wondered if you people would like to have milk deliveries started to your apartment."

"Oh, no, thank you."

"You folks new in town?"

"Yes, we are—enrolled to go to Multnomah School of

the Bible as soon as it opens."

He smiled. "You must be Christians."

"Yes, we are."

They talked a while. The man said, "I'm a Gideon here in town. We'll be meeting in a couple of days. I'd like you to meet some of the Christians in town." He started off and then came back. "Here—even if you're not going to take milk—here's a quart of milk and some cottage cheese, compliments of the dairy."

One day they found a bag of groceries outside their door, left by some anonymous benefactor. They felt that the Lord was watching over them, day by day. During these days, it seemed that they were always hungry. They would stroll into supermarkets and try all the food samples that were being given away, then walk to the next grocery. Those were days of learning about their Saviour and the meaning of dedication to Him that never left them.

Soon Bill was taking a full schedule at Multnomah School of the Bible. The need for jobs to cover expenses was greater than ever. Barbara faithfully continued to look for work. Bill would meet her as she got off the bus, looking so tired and dejected. In New York City she had seldom sensed any danger or fear. She'd always felt like the same little girl from Napoleon, Ohio, until now in Portland, Oregon. She told Bill afterward, "That's where I grew up in a hurry."

Gordon Mohr and his wife, Beverly, arrived. His plans had changed also. He had decided to accept the offer to take complete charge of a dismal little downtown Christian bookstore which was owned by Multnomah. In the years to follow, this store was to grow and develop a healthy group of branch stores and to become a wholesale as well as retail outlet for Christian publications.

Years later, Multnomah School of the Bible, in announcing the construction of a new all-purpose gym and activities building, would print in their annual report for 1972:

> In His marvelous providence, God allowed a wholesale book business to be developed under the expert business leadership of Gordon Mohr, who was employed by the school. The recent sale of this thriving business and ministry to Tyndale House has brought this year to the Building Fund a total of $250,000.

Eventually Bill got a part-time job with an electrical firm in Portland. The hours would not interfere with his classes. His delight in having work at last was tempered somewhat by the discovery that in addition to warehouse work, he would be delivering parts all over a strange town in a vintage panel truck. The first time he sat in this vehicle and reached under the steering wheel for the automatic transmission control, he found none. Instead, off to his right, there was a little black sphere the size of a golf ball which topped a mysterious rod going down through the floor. He remembered vaguely from his childhood in Waxahachie that this was a stick shift and was used in conjunction with a clutch for shifting gears. He was shaken badly enough to risk the embarrassment of telling his new boss that he couldn't drive with a stick shift.

His boss seemed quite unshaken by this bit of news.

"You drive, don't you? I mean, you can handle the rest of it? I suppose you have a driver's license."

"Well, yes."

"That's fine. We've got a teen-ager here who'll give you a lesson or two."

After some time, Bill hurt his back lifting something heavy on the job. Bedridden for several days, he knew that he had to look for other work.

10

The job which opened up for Bill and Barbara was to take care of a thirty-five-year-old woman who was incapacitated by multiple sclerosis. Her name was Helen. She'd been a sorority girl in college, a socialite, and was married to a handsome young husband who disappeared as soon as the disease began to take its toll on her physically. Her family was wealthy; money was not the problem—keeping anybody to take care of her for more than a few days was the problem. She was wearing diapers, her eyesight was going and she could not control the violent trembling of her legs and hands. Her reaction to all this was to scream and to lash out at anybody near her.

Bill and Barbara took the job. Now they were living amid luxury, with the best of food. There was a gardener to do the yard work, a housekeeper to clean the rooms and a trained masseur came regularly to give treatments. They had the run of the house, with the nicest bedroom of their married lives to that point. The only rooms Helen frequented were her own room and the kitchen where she was taken in a wheelchair for one meal each day. They had an open charge account for groceries. Nevertheless, they soon learned why nobody would stay very long in that house.

Helen was unreasonable in her demands; she lashed out at them almost constantly, screaming and abusing them as they tried their best to help her. It was necessary to use a lifting basket to get her from her bed into her wheelchair and then back into bed. Trying to move her and to clean her body were nerve-racking tasks. Barbara broke out in great welts just from nerves. They began to feel stifled in that place. Sometimes they imagined they heard Helen walking in the halls at night: knowing that she could not walk made it the more frightening. They knew that Helen had gone through several cults and religions and it seemed that Satan was master in that house.

When this became too much to bear any longer, Bill spoke to Helen. In a strong, confident tone, he assured her that he and Barbara loved her—that more important, God loved her. He said, "We've come here to take care of you and we will. But while we're here, we won't allow you to scream at us and treat us so harshly."

This firm approach seemed the right one. Helen relaxed noticeably. She knew that Bill was studying for the ministry. He and Barbara began to read the Bible and to pray with Helen every day. They told her that Jesus loved her and they prayed that He would give her peace. After that, the situation was more bearable, though it was still very difficult. Once a week another girl came to care for her, while they took refuge in a quiet little basement room or went to stay with friends.

Soon they were able to make a down payment on a 1953 Chevrolet. This proved to be a good little car and they were able to get around the area during weekends for the speaking opportunities that opened up. Bill and Barbara rehearsed one of the playlets Bill had written while at Dallas. It was a simple little story about a Christian college girl and her boyfriend who had gone away into the navy. After many trying situations, he, too, finds the Lord. It wasn't great theater, yet it carried a strong message and they acted their parts with skill and appeal. Due to word of mouth, performances were in frequent demand. One man wrote, "This is the most beautiful presentation of the gospel that I have ever seen."

One day they were asked to go to an honor camp for delinquent boys who had been sent to a reformatory near Seaside. Upon arrival they were told, "This is really a bad day for a speaker. It's the one day when they are allowed a few hours of freedom to go into town—to see a movie, go bowling or something like that. They'll resent hearing a lecture during their free time."

That day, the men who worked in camp with these youngsters saw something exciting happen that they could hardly believe. When Bill began to talk, the boys gave him their complete attention. When he talked over-time and they knew that they were freed by the clock to go for their fun, they stayed a whole hour later. When they were challenged to receive Christ, thirty of them did so in an open decision.

When Barbara and Bill were free to do so, they went to every meeting at which they had been invited to speak. Sometimes they drove their little Chevy for hundreds of miles and the five dollars—or nothing—they received caused anxiety and prayer that they'd get home without running out of gas. Bill was learning quickly that to mention money "was not Christian." They sometimes drove wearying miles to beautiful places where they noticed many obviously well-to-do people, yet they received less than the bare expenses of travel for their ministry.

One night, after such a meeting, Bill opened the envelope handed to him so ceremoniously and found five dollars within. He got so angry that he cursed. God dealt with Bill that night. The shock of his own outburst helped him to realize that his attitude was completely out of fellowship with his Lord. God made it clear to him that he was not employed by men at these meetings, but that as Jesus had taught, he was to look to the heavenly Father, giver of every perfect gift. He would supply their needs —if not here, then in some other way.

Near the end of the school year, Barbara told Bill that she was expecting their first child. They were frightened, yet excited and happy. Together, they began to pray and to plan for this little son who would be born to them. They knew that it was going to be a boy. Bill had told Barbara that *they* wanted a boy, and she wanted very much to please him.

There were many problems and little emergencies in connection with caring for Helen. Very soon Barbara ought not to be doing the lifting the work required. Bill realized that she should be in a more relaxed atmosphere during her pregnancy. With this in mind, they prayed for guidance.

Bill didn't know what to do next. He must find a place of peace and safety for Barbara. They had been attending a little log church with stained-glass windows. It was called The Chapel of the Hills and had been founded by Thyra Strand, whose husband, Al, was a real-estate man. Thyra's family had homesteaded the land round about. Here Al, a very personable Christian fellow, had built a lovely home with an adjoining apartment for speakers or visiting missionaries who came to the church. The Strands had been observing Barbara and Bill and now they invited them to live in the apartment. Bill would be youth director for the chapel and also work as custodian. Thyra had a green thumb. Along ledges in the sanctuary and throughout the church were dozens of potted ivy plants she had planted. It would also be Bill's responsibility to water these, keeping them fresh and green. A modest salary was included in the agreement. Bill would also have time to study and attend classes.

Here in the last few weeks before Barbara's child was due, they experienced such peace as they had never known since their marriage. Bill worked in the yard and performed happily the simple chores which were important, plus ministering to a group of wonderful kids. Barbara laughed as she told Bill, "I'm not going to have this baby on a weekend because that would mess up your youth ministry."

They went to bed after the Sunday activities of October 15, 1961. Sometime after midnight, she scratched his back to wake him up and said, "Bill, I think I'm going to have the baby tonight."

"Oh, Barbara!" He leapt out of bed like a volunteer fireman and threw on his clothes. Barbara was dressing very calmly in her best maternity clothes. While Bill rushed upstairs to tell Thyra and Al, Barbara put on her makeup very carefully. The astonished Bill was certain that no girl had ever been so at peace about having a baby.

It was a foggy night in the mountain foothills and Bill crept along the road, concerned lest he hit a deer and injure Barbara. Arriving at the hospital, Barbara was so pretty and so composed that the nurse teased her, "You're going to have a baby? You just think you are!" They allowed Bill in the labor room, where he sat by her bed and rubbed her back. He loved her so much! They prayed together and he could hardly take in the wonder of what was happening. The nurses kept checking Barbara. They remarked about her beautiful spirit as they wheeled her into the delivery room.

Thyra kept Bill company as he stood waiting. Soon they heard the cry of a new life and they both wept with joy as little Stephen Thomas Roberts was born. When it was time to take him home, they realized that they knew nothing about the care and feeding of a new baby. They were scared to wash him; Bill was afraid he'd break in two when he picked him up. The ladies of the neighborhood offered all kinds of advice, like, "Of course you're going to nurse him, Barbara."

"Why, of course," she said, and she tried so hard. Little Stephen cried a lot. This frightened his inexperienced parents. One person said, "Let him cry it out and go to sleep." Another said, "Pick him up, of course." Then no matter what they did, they feared it was the wrong thing and they worried. Bill was so concerned about the baby that he neglected his work cleaning the church. He forgot to water the plants until some of them died. Then he realized that this was not living a good testimony for Christ.

One night Bill and Barbara were working together cleaning one of the rest rooms and they both began to laugh because God had brought them along such a strange path to serve Him. Bill said, "Do you remember when we were dating in New York City and we were looking up at Manhattan Towers? I had friends there and they had maids and, oh, it was so beautiful and I said, 'One day, Barbara, we're going to live in a place like that!' Now we're cleaning rest rooms out in the country outside Portland, Oregon!"

She said, "Oh, I never really cared much for glamorous things. We've got Stephen and I'm happy."

They had a happy relationship with the church members and with the young people, many of whom came to know the Lord. The Strands had been good to them. Thyra was a real scholar of the Word of God. She was respected highly by the professors at Multnomah and the pastors in Portland who knew her. Through her teaching, Bill had learned a great deal of doctrine, and through her life and that of her husband, he had had consistent examples of mature Christian living. He felt so thankful for the solid foundation her teaching had given him in the Christian life. They had been so good to his little family, acting more like loving grandparents than superiors.

Bill completed his year at Multnomah. After loving farewells, they left the Chapel of the Hills and started on a tour. Bill realized later that this wasn't very practical. He had a young wife and a four-months-old baby. The little fellow had done so well on their first travels to speak and Bill was not concerned.

Quite unknown to Bill, he was entering into a year of suffering, weakness and defeat—the ebb tide of his life. Near Bakersfield, his birthplace, he unknowingly contracted what is known as San Joaquin Valley fever, caused by an obscure but deadly fungus inhaled into the lungs.

Approaching Dallas, he was unable to continue his journey and ended up flat on his back in his mother's home. Ordered to a strict regimen of bed rest, he was unable to support his wife and child. Though his mother understood and was glad to have him home, other relatives and family friends saw him lying around the house, looking perfectly well, and spread the word that Bill Roberts was plumb lazy. One of them said, "Bill, you've failed at everything you've ever tried."

In his depression and weakness, Bill accepted this as true enough. He had failed Barbara and little Stephen— worst of all, he had failed his Lord. He said to her, "I've really bottomed out. I can't get lower than this."

Barbara began to sing to him, "What a Friend we have in Jesus. . . . We should never be discouraged. . . . Take it to the Lord in prayer." Bill burst into sobs and as she put her arms around him, the unbearable tension was released. From that day his health improved.

During this period, Bill had written to all his old contacts about the possibility of a national tour. He wrote to the Stonecroft Ministries in Kansas City, Missouri, whose work included Christian Women's Clubs, Village Missions and Christian Business and Professional Councils and Couples' Clubs. He wrote to others, too, including Youth for Christ and Christian Business Men's Committee. He wanted to include all of them in a tour he was planning. Bill's brother, Tommy, was quite excited about all this. He had been disturbed and concerned as he watched his older brother become so defeated and discouraged.

Before the weekend arrived, Bill received a letter from Mrs. Helen Baugh, one of the founders of Christian Women's Clubs. She invited him to come to Kansas City to talk about a tour. Mrs. Baugh and her co-founder, Miss Mary Clark, had read the *Decision* article about Bill. They did an unusual thing for their organization: offered to pay his bus fare.

Stonecroft was the name of the lovely old estate the founders had bought for a residence and administrative headquarters of their work. Mrs. Baugh called it holy ground, and Bill sensed that the Spirit of the living God was there. The whole place had a different atmosphere and the workers a different attitude from what he had expected. It became obvious to him that all there had dedicated their lives to serving the Lord. There were differences in personalities here but no clashing of egos.

Shortly after his arrival, Bill was invited to tea in the main building of the old mansion where many of the staff lived.

Miss Clark and Mrs. Baugh began to talk about their

work with Village Missions, which was supported through nationwide Christian Women's Clubs and their other affilliated groups.

Mary Clark threw him her curve ball. She said, "Do you know what our project is, Bill? The only project of Christian Women's Clubs is sending couples out into rural America—into little country churches."

When he got home and greeted Barbara, he had to sit down before he could bring himself to tell her. "Barbara, guess what they want us to be. They want us to be village missionaries! Can you imagine that?"

Barbara jumped up and hugged him close. She said, "Oh, Bill, that's wonderful! I knew that I couldn't stay on the road with you and we'd be headed for long separations. I'm just thrilled."

His mother came close to doing a dance, she was so happy. Another prayer had been answered.

11

Bill and Barbara packed their belongings for their trip to Kansas City and several weeks of indoctrination at Stonecroft. After a visit to Barbara's family in Ohio, they started for Washington State.

Two thousand miles later, they crossed the Cascade Range through Stevens Pass and came down the valley to the little pioneer town of Snohomish. A service station owner directed them to a country road. Machias was six miles north. Driving left and right on gravel roads, they reached the church. The architecture was typically New England, clean lines dominated by the steeple. Even in the dark it had the run-down look of long neglect.

The parsonage was next door, they had been told. They drove next door to find a dismal little shack of a parsonage, trimmed with black paint, like an old-fashioned funeral notice.

Word spread quickly that the new preacher and his family had arrived. A few minutes later they were inside the little parsonage, more or less in a state of shock, travel weary and Barbara many months pregnant—with the door opening constantly as people crowded into that little place to greet them and, as Bill suspected, to size them up.

During the next five and a half years, many of the people who crowded into the little parsonage that first night would become firm friends.

The church was heated by a large wood burning furnace, aided by two oil stoves. A huge pile of logs, bucked to furnace length, was stacked between church and parsonage. That was the loggers' part of the heating responsibility. From then on, it was in the hands of the village missionary.

Bill's first sermon topic was *Love.* He sat in the pulpit waiting to preach. He remembered something said back at Village Missions headquarters. "Go into that little parsonage, put on the coffeepot and *love those people!*"

Bill preached his sermon on love. No matter what the subject, it probably would have been a difficult morning, not only for him and for Barbara, but for the congregation. He sensed their reaction to be, *He's an outsider, a city fellow. We wish him well, but we'll wait and see how he turns out.*

This was the unlikely start of a five-and-a-half-year ministry in Machias Community Church. Forty to fifty people gathered for Sunday morning services. Eighteen was a good number in the evening service at the beginning and four to nine souls at midweek Bible study. They sat close to the big wood stove because the church was so chilly. The church had a nucleus of mature Christians who sustained Bill and Barbara during the breaking-in period. Bill recognized the breaking, all right. That was his back.

Through all this, Bill and Barbara never ceased to pray for the church. Bill knew that his ministry couldn't be based on drama or dramatic programs. He would only be trying to top himself each week. The way to draw men was to uphold Christ. Bill began to preach through the Bible. He started a planned course in Bible memory work. Nine started and at one time sixty people were taking this course. The sanctuary began to fill up Sunday mornings. Members brought their guests and new people were coming.

Right in the beginning, Bill had written a long letter to his mother. He told her how much he loved her and thanked her for praying him into this country church. He told her he was struggling with problems but had great peace and felt that he and Barbara were really in the place where God wanted them.

A few weeks later, he got a telephone call from Waxahachie. "Bill, your mother has died very suddenly. We couldn't even warn you. Come home for the funeral."

He could hardly believe what had happened. His mother was an active, vital woman, just turned sixty a few days before. He had naturally expected her to live on for years. Now he remembered her saying, "I feel something wonderful is going to happen." His mother's prayers had been completely answered. He was pastor of a little country church and even its color was what she had prayed for: white.

Now there was a quietness in his leadership. He felt that the people should get much more involved. When a class needed a teacher, he told the people of the need and said, "It's better for a Sunday-school class to dissolve than to have a teacher who is not God's choice." When they thought this strange and felt that they should coerce somebody into leadership, Bill said, "God is more interested in His work than we are. We must not shove a person into a job. If God's choice is here, He will burden that heart and we'll have a volunteer."

Barbara and Bill had prayed for children. Stephen had come to them twenty-three months after their marriage and another child had been conceived during the hard year in Waxahachie. The home folks didn't seem too excited over the prospect at the time when very little was going well for the young couple. After arriving in Machias early in September, they were really excited. September 30, 1963, was a Sunday, and it didn't look as if Barbara would carry her baby into October as the doctor expected. That morning she told Bill, "I'm not going to interfere with your Sunday services." She kept her word: late that night, they sang together between the labor pains, all the way to the hospital at Arlington, sixteen miles away.

When they arrived, the nurse said, "Oh, my! This is going to be a long, long time." Bill held Barbara in his arms and they prayed, "Oh dear Lord, you can help this new little baby to come easily—and let it come quickly."

A few minutes later the nurse came in casually to check Barbara. She gasped, "I can't believe it! The baby is almost here!" She ran out and gave the doctor an urgent call. He came running into the hospital and they wheeled Barbara into delivery. Little Philip Roberts was born almost immediately. Barbara said that when he was born she was perfectly conscious—taking a few whiffs of gas to ease the pain—and while he was being born, she literally saw stars.

Standing just outside the door, Bill heard the first cry of little Philip, born just twenty-three months after his brother, Stephen. The two brothers looked quite different. Stephen was blond and blue-eyed. Philip had his father's olive complexion. His eyes were green and they soon saw that he was to have wiry brown hair. He was a happy baby and a joy to all.

Just twenty-three months later, their third little boy, David, was born. Now Bill and Barbara thought that they had the perfect family. They were very protective of these children; they hardly ever let anyone else keep them. They were careful about things like vitamins and were frightened by the rough play some of the church children would get them into. But the boys seemed to thrive and grow so fast. Stephen and Philip loved to go to the church with Daddy to help him get ready for communion services. They often entertained him from the church platform—"just for Daddy." It seemed that wherever he went, one or both little boys tagged along behind. Philip began to talk early and Stephen also was a bright little boy.

Bill was extremely strict with his children. He thought that preachers' children were supposed to set a good example. This could make things difficult. As the eldest, Stephen sometimes got the brunt of Bill's criticism.

One morning when they were a bit late getting next door to Sunday school, Stephen insisted on taking a very noisy toy with him. Instead of behaving like a wise adult,

Bill lost his temper. He grabbed the toy away from Stephen, threw it into the toy box and jerked Stephen almost through the air. As they opened the door, Stephen was weeping and pulling back. Bill was glaring at his son, but the moment he closed the door behind them, he put on his pious pastor's face and smiled at the parishioners who were arriving. Then he dragged little Stephen off to Sunday school. Bill had his class in a room adjoining Stephen's and through the thin partition he could hear the teenager having her difficulties with his little son and knew that his daddy was to blame.

Every now and then the sermon topic, carefully prepared though it invariably was, could prove by Sunday morning to be a sword in the breast of the preacher. Bill knew that he couldn't preach about "The Victorious Christian Life." Was he a victorious Christian father? He felt convicted in his heart and asked the Lord's forgiveness. Right after Sunday school he began looking for Stephen. He found his little blond son walking dejectedly across the vacant lot between church and parsonage, going to get his mother and baby brother for church. Bill ran after him and knelt beside him and put his arms around him.

"Stephen, Daddy was wrong, jerking your toy away and shouting at you. Will you forgive Daddy?"

He said, "Sure, Daddy," and he hugged his father around the neck and kissed him. Before his sermon, Bill shared his parental failure and there were tears of identification all across the church. After this, Bill gave up all pretense of being the perfect pastor. He shared personal experiences of failure. He asked, "How many of you fought in the car all the way to church, then when you stepped out, suddenly put on your church smile?" They laughed. Then he said, "When we go home from the Lord's house and close the door and pull the shades and shed our Christian saintliness like a coat—then we are not living a victorious life, and the glowing testimonies that we give here are just a mockery."

They began to realize that while their pastor had come from a very different part of the country and was strange to some of their ways and work, he was not living in an ivory tower. He was just a man seeking to do the will of God—but apart from God he could do nothing of value for Him. There began to grow a loving understanding between pastor and people.

The Lord brought warm love and dignity to the church at Machias. Souls were saved who had been prayed for years before the Robertses arrived. The church family was growing and it was time to do something about the physical condition of the church.

By now it was obvious to the church board that if the growth they were experiencing were to be continued, they would need to make some sensible long-range plans and then step out in faith. In addition to substantial repairs to the church, the parsonage was surveyed and found to be in such a state of decay that it would need to be torn down and a new one built on the same site—or else another home purchased for use as a parsonage.

Adjoining the church was a sixty-foot lot, privately owned by a man who refused to sell. Bill told the board that an undesirable building that close to the church could prove disastrous. They began to pray and the man who owned the lot came to them of his own accord and asked, "Weren't you interested in buying that lot?" So they bought it for future expansion.

On the corner lot in this same block was an attractive, well-built house, bordered by large eastern maple trees. It was owned by a widow who had been a prominent resident of Machias. All her children were college graduates and had gone elsewhere into excellent jobs. Mrs. Barrows was a cultured person, personable and highly intelligent. She had dipped into various religions and cults and had never felt secure in any abiding faith in Jesus Christ.

One of her best friends died and Bill was asked to break the news to the old lady. Bill knew that her friend was a Christian. He was to hold the funeral service a day or two later. So he told Mrs. Barrows that her friend was now with the Lord.

She asked, "How can you be so sure?"

He shared with her the simple gospel. She had heard it before in the church, yet it seemed that now for the first time her understanding was receptive to the Spirit of God.

"I want to be absolutely sure. I'm an old woman and I've been searching all my life for something I could hold to and really trust."

He said, "You can be sure. Just ask Jesus into your heart." Then with the simplicity of a child, this intelligent old lady asked Christ to forgive all her sins and to come into her heart.

From that day, Mrs. Barrows began to witness to people throughout the community that she had been born again. They had long known of her explorations into religions. Now she told them of the certainty of her peace with God.

Soon afterward, Mrs. Barrows suffered a severe stroke which left her speechless and completely paralyzed. Word came to Bill that she was a human vegetable and that there was no point in his visiting her. Nevertheless, he went to the nursing home where she lay motionless with tubes in her nose. He was told that she understood nothing, yet he felt strongly urged to try to communicate.

"Mrs. Barrows, I'm here and I know how much you love Jesus." He began to quote Bible verses. Her eyes were open and fixed upon him. Then Bill noticed that every time there was a sound from the hall, her eyes moved toward the sound. He thought, She's not a vegetable. Her body can't move, but she hears every word. She just can't communicate. This encouraged him and he continued to talk to her in a loving way as if she heard perfectly, and he quoted verses which he believed would be comforting and assuring.

Then he noticed that she was moving one hand just a little and he said, "Mrs. Barrows, I know you have difficulty in moving, but if you've heard everything I've said, will you please slide your hand into mine."

Bill placed his open palm beside her frail little hand and soon it raised just a bit and slowly moved over and dropped into his. He rejoiced; she had heard. Then he thought of the people who had said in her presence that she was a vegetable. The sadness and frustration she must have experienced because nobody considered it of any use to visit her! Bill came to see her almost every day and spread the word so that her old neighbors came and talked to her.

When Mrs. Barrows died, Bill shared her story—how in love he had talked to her about Jesus, and she had found, so late in life, the Friend who would never leave or forsake her. The relatives were greatly comforted and asked for a copy of the message.

The house on the corner, priced at nine thousand dollars and appraised at more, was up for sale with several prospective purchasers. The deacons discussed the challenge, their problem of money, and prayed about it. Nine thousand dollars seemed a tremendous sum, especially when the sanctuary needed extensive repairs. Borrowing money seemed unwise. This house—just what they needed—was beyond their reach.

While they were still discussing this problem, the phone rang. One of the sons said, "The family has decided to let the church have the property for four thousand dollars, and we'll leave the piano in it."

Thus they were able to begin active repairs on the church building. The first job was to reshake the church roof. After they had let the contract to a roofer, they learned that he was also doing several other jobs under contract and they thought he would never get the church roof on again before the rains set in.

This roofer had an inspiration to save time and trouble. He said, "I'm going to cut five feet off that steeple."

Bill said, "Sir, you must not cut *one inch* off that steeple.

You'll destroy the look of the church."

"But it's dangerous up there."

Bill said, "Well, sir, if you fall from five feet below the top, you'll kill yourself anyway. Just be careful. I'm going inside and pray for you—it's too scary to watch. But don't you dare cut one inch off that steeple."

The roofer and his men built a scaffold around the steeple and shaped it up to the tip. Part of the contract was to put a brass ball on the very tip of the steeple. On the last day, Bill asked the roofer, "What in the world are you putting on top?"

The man was holding one of those large balls of heavy plastic that little children love to play with. There were butterflies and all sorts of other goodies spinning around within. The roofer sprayed it with several coats of gold paint, remarking, "You won't have to polish this one." He attached it firmly to the top of the Machias Community Church steeple, where it remains to this day.

The next job was to plaster the interior of the church. The Sunday after this job was contracted for, Bill said to the congregation, "Dear people, will you join me in prayer? We had so much difficulty getting the roof on, let's pray that our church will get plastered to the honor and glory of God." Then in the middle of his pastoral prayer, he heard snickers sweeping across the pews and realized what he had said.

Interest in the church spread far beyond Machias. A beautiful painting of the renovated church graced the Christmas card sent out that year by the Everett *Herald*, newspaper of the county seat. It made the front cover of

the Seattle *Times Sunday Magazine*—the New England-
style church, freshly painted white, with the gold ball atop
its tall steeple, framed in evergreen trees with the Cascade mountains in the background. Don Duncan, a writer
from the *Seattle Times*, called for an interview with
photos. A few days later, in Vancouver, B. C., on a speaking engagement, Bill was passing a newsstand and
stopped in astonishment as his eye caught a large picture
of him with Barbara and their three little boys. He had
never dreamed that their story would be considered significant enough for a page-one story, yet there it was.

Next came a call from United Press International. Bill
and Barbara were still hurriedly tidying the parsonage
and getting the three boys in fresh clothes when a modest
car drove up and "O. K." Boyington came into their lives
"for just forty-five minutes," but stayed more than two
hours and became a friend. His story and pictures went all
over the United States.

Then a syndicated columnist called from Chicago to do
still another story, to be published nationwide, about an
ex-actor who became a country preacher. In a way, all this
was encouraging—even gratifying—yet it left Bill with a
sober sense of responsibility to his Lord. As for the little
Community Church at Machias, it was getting difficult for
latecomers to find a seat. And back at Stonecroft there was
no longer any talk about closing down that church in the
place which wasn't on the map.

12

Bill and Barbara took their three little boys on a vacation trip to visit Barbara's mother and father in Ohio. Stephen was nearly six, Philip nearly four and David would be two in August.

They had a wonderful visit and then headed west again for Machias. When they were nearly a hundred miles from Missoula, Montana, Philip became violently ill with stomach cramps and began screaming in pain. He was so pale and trembling that his parents were panic-stricken. As they entered each small settlement along the road and asked at service stations or country stores where they could find a doctor, the answer was always, "No doctor here. The nearest doctor's in Missoula." They prayed aloud as they drove, Barbara holding Philip and doing all in her power to comfort him.

On the outskirts of Missoula, they saw a police officer and asked for help. He led them to a doctor, who examined Philip the best he could in his office.

"We'll have to hospitalize this little fellow," the doctor said. "It could be appendicitis; it could be food poisoning —or something else. You can't fool around with something like this."

They took little Philip to the Missoula hospital; he seemed so desperately ill. Bill phoned Stonecroft and asked them to pray.

The next morning, Philip seemed perfectly well and was released from the hospital. "We're pretty certain it was not appendicitis," the doctor said. "Whatever it is— or was—I'd keep an eye on him and take him to your doctor for another check as soon as you get back to Washington State."

After reaching Machias, Bill and Barbara took Philip to a physician and surgeon in nearby Arlington. He checked Philip carefully, but found nothing wrong. From time to time, Philip experienced abdominal pain and cried out, "My tummy, oh, my tummy!" He'd been checked by doctors so many times and the spasms always seemed to pass. Then Barbara's brother, Ted, came to visit and they ate together at a restaurant. Once again, Philip had a serious attack—much like the first one in Montana—so they rushed to Arlington again. As they had eaten out, the doctor thought it might be food poisoning. Bill and Barbara decided that Philip must have a sensitive stomach or be allergic to some foods. After this, some time passed with no further attacks.

One Saturday night, Barbara called Bill into the boys' bedroom where the three little fellows were sleeping. "Look at their stomachs—compare them, Bill. Now look again at Philip's abdomen; it's hard and rigid."

Bill checked with gentle fingers. Barbara was right; there was a difference. So they took Philip to the doctor once more, explaining what they had noticed. Even as he was looking, the doctor said, "I wish you'd go to a pediatrician. Don't delay."

They took him to young Dr. Leslie Nelson in Everett. That morning, while Barbara was dressing Philip for the trip, he sang in his clear treble voice, "I don't care about tomorrow. I just live from day to day." He sang almost all the words of the song.

Dr. Nelson checked Philip very carefully. His quiet words that followed cut deep into their hearts.

"Bill, Barbara, I'm almost certain that Philip has cancer."

They sat there numb as the dreaded words sank in. They were the sort of parents who could hardly read about other suffering children. Then their minds rushed back to all the times Philip had screamed in pain. Time, time, relentless time had been ticking on with this horrible bomb growing inside their Philip.

Through their daze they heard Dr. Nelson's voice, kind but insistent. "There's only one place for this little boy—Children's Orthopedic Hospital in Seattle. You must take him at once! I'll phone ahead."

That night Philip's parents learned what it means to be grief-stricken. They both felt literally ill from shock. Barbara said she felt like she did when giving birth. Bill had nothing in his experience to compare with this surging and cutting and pounding of his very soul.

Philip was delighted. "We're going on a special trip to Seattle. Stephen and David don't get to go, but I do." Yes, it was a very special trip indeed. It was a trip through the valley of the shadow whose effects would reach to the other side of the world. None of them knew this at the time. It was a dark December evening of 1966 and in the blessed darkness the happy little boy could not see the flood of tears that soaked the front of his parents' clothing as they drove south. They had dedicated Philip to the Lord before he was born and they knew that God, who was not the author of sin, disease or death, loved this child of their bodies more than they. They knew all this, but they were not experiencing an hour of triumph through their risen Saviour; they were deep in the dread valley.

They didn't know how to explain to a little three-year-old boy that he was to be taken from their arms by people in white clothing and whisked away into the depths of a great hospital. They did get an impression of remarkable kindness in spite of the calm professional speed with which the waiting experts took charge. Except for one night in the Missoula hospital, Philip had never been away from them. Now they prayed with him, then had to tear themselves away and stand helpless as they heard him crying after them, "Mommy—Daddy, come back!"

Barbara and Bill sobbed all the way home to Machias. Doom smothered their minds. They knew that unless God performed a miracle, their dear Philip was bound down a horrifying path to a pain-racked death. In the darkness of their bed, they called out to God for pity and mercy and for the miracle of healing for their precious child. From time to time they awoke from fitful sleep, clinging to each other and sobbing with a bitter sense of desolation.

When they returned to Orthopedic Hospital the next day, Lucille Hedeen, a dear friend, was holding Philip on her lap. She and Philip had a very special relationship. He had said to her once, "I'm going to marry you when I grow up."

And she accepted. She said, "I'm going to wait for you, Philip." Now she held him and talked with him as the doctors beckoned to Bill and Barbara. Surgery was scheduled for one o'clock the next day. They would do a biopsy then, but the diagnosis, almost certainly, was either Wiems's tumor or neuroblastoma. They were told kindly but frankly that only a small percentage of children ever recovered. Once again, night came and they were asked to leave Philip.

Sleep was nearly impossible that night. They got up early, planning to reach the hospital by nine o'clock, in plenty of time to visit with Philip before his surgery. While they were dressing, the phone rang. When Bill answered, somebody said, "We are taking Philip into surgery."

Bill almost screamed, "But you said it would be one o'clock. You promised us and we haven't seen him!" He felt like shouting, "You can't do that; you can't do that!"

They were going to do that. They would attend to Philip's need with the highest skills in the nation and they had charge of the emergency. Bill realized all this as the surgeon said very quietly, but with positive authority, "We must take him in right now."

Soon after they reached the hospital to begin the long wait during surgery, Dr. Robert Brown, pastor of Westminster Church in Everett, arrived with his wife, Adelaide. They enveloped the troubled young parents with their love and then led them from the hospital to have a bite to eat. This was the first of many times that the Bob Browns appeared beside them at that hospital, smiling love and encouragement. For several years the Roberts family had spent every Christmas Day at the Browns', opening their presents there. Bob and Adelaide seemed like grandparents to their three boys and now they shared in their grief.

Philip was four-and-one-half hours in surgery. A massive malignant tumor had been removed and it had been necessary also to do a nephrectomy. The cancer had spread to the lymph glands. The diagnosis was neuroblastoma, a highly malignant tumor of the nerve cells of the abdomen, probably arising from the central portion of the adrenal gland. This in turn had involved the kidney, upon which it rested. They were told that this tumor, which is usually confined to children under four years old, had grown rapidly to a very large size. As a Christian doctor explained, without divine intervention, either Wiems's or neuroblastoma tumors are invariably fatal.

Children's Orthopedic Hospital, the only one of its kind for many states around, is a center whose devoted staff have the most advanced knowledge and provide the utmost in skilled treatment for the various dreaded cancers of children. The people here would do everything humanly possible for Philip. Yet it became clear to Barbara and to Bill that the only really effective avenue open to them was intercessory prayer.

The word went out and soon across the entire nation, from Texas to Ohio, from New York to California, Oregon

FROM MAKE-BELIEVE TO REALITY   127

and Washington State, family and Christian friends, on hearing the dread news, pleaded with the Lord in behalf of little Philip Roberts. Those who knew and loved this endearing and promising little boy prayed for him. They prayed in groups gathered in churches and in homes. They prayed individually while driving in cars and while lying in their beds. They did not demand this of God, but begged that in His mercy and power and knowledge of all things, He would return little Philip to health and his full boyish strength. Most of all, almost every conscious moment of their days and nights, Bill and Barbara prayed. As they prayed, loving their God, they knew that His best answer might be no. They submitted themselves to the discipline of God's will, but this came hard and only from aching hearts, after a flood of tears.

Toward the end of this most difficult of days, while Philip was still in recovery, Lucille Hedeen came up to them again and asked what they were planning to do overnight.

"We'll stay as long as we can and then drive back to Machias until morning," Bill said. "There's Stephen and David. . . ."

"You know they're in good hands," Lucille said. "They're probably having fun and getting spoiled rotten. You'll just wear yourselves out driving back and forth the next few days."

"Oh, thanks, but we can make it all right. We are awfully tired. . . ."

"Listen, there's a couple almost across the street who've invited you to come stay overnight with them anytime.

Let me introduce you. They're waiting down the hall."
Lucille nearly dragged them to the lobby, where for the
first time Bill and Barbara met Winston and Irma Johnson.

The Johnsons gave them a key to their house and put
them up in a bedroom with a window looking right up to
where Philip was. "This is your home now—just come and
go as you please." These dear people tempted their appe-
tites with Scandinavian holiday goodies and steaming
coffee. "We want you to be happy here—as much as you
can be happy," Irma told them.

Philip was on the critical list off and on during a span
of five weeks. During this time Bill and Barbara came to
realize that they belonged to a veritable fraternity of parents whose children were in that hospital, suffering from
various types of cancer and other desperate illnesses.
With these other parents they shared a fellowship of suffering. The Children's Orthopedic Hospital, begun in 1907
as a seven-bed ward and now a two-hundred-bed hospital
in its own beautiful building, had never had a chaplain.
Soon Bill was wandering down the halls meeting children
who were frightfully ill or injured. He was impressed with
their bravery and then by their loneliness. Some had
come from Alaska or Idaho and were far from family or
playmates. Some had working parents who came when
they could to sit by their bedsides. Bill found there were
things he could do to bring a measure of happiness into
the weary and pain-filled hours of these precious children.

He did a funny reading for a boy with leukemia. His
parents said, "That's the first time he's laughed since he's
been here."

One little girl was terrified at the prospect of being left alone by her parents for the first night in her life. Her mother was so concerned; she couldn't think of any way to comfort her child. Bill went in and took the child's hand in his. He said to her, "Honey, you're not going to be alone. Jesus is going to be with you when your Mommy goes and you don't need to be afraid anymore." She let her mother go that night without crying. The anxious mother could hardly believe the peace which had entered her little girl's heart.

Bill was learning to be sensitive to the parents. He learned that as a stranger, he couldn't rush upon people —in grief over their children—who doubted the ability of anybody else to really understand. One day he saw a young couple who had just learned that their little child was dying of a brain tumor. In their extreme frustration of grief they were ready to tear the hospital and staff apart, and Bill knew that emotion himself. When he approached them carefully, anxious to comfort, yet not intrude, they looked up at him in anger.

Bill said softly, "I've just heard about your child and I want you to know I do understand. Our little boy is just two doors away from him. The doctors say we shouldn't expect him to live very long. I just want to tell you that in the midst of our sorrow, we've found such peace with God. It's the only peace we've found here."

The child's mother looked up and said in a shaken voice and in tears, "Do you know that just a few minutes ago I said, 'I hate God. If my child dies, I'm going to hate Him forever!' "

Bill said, "I understand your feeling, but it's not God who is the author of this. He's the only one who can bring peace to your heart."

The next day this mother found Bill in the hall. She grasped his hand and said, "You're right. He is the only peace in the middle of all this." And through her tears, this time she was smiling.

There were brave children in that hospital. Youngsters with half their small bodies encased in plaster casts worked cheerfully with whatever muscles they were able to use. Some dragged themselves along nursery floors, playing almost like children with healthy bodies. Bill met one teen-age girl who showed such courage and laughed so heartily while already crippled with a lethal type of cancer that he was amazed and became one of her admirers and sharers of small jokes. He learned that it was just as important—and sometimes even more difficult—to share laughter as to share tears.

A front-page news story was done about Philip. The article stated that Bill was the unofficial chaplain of the Children's Orthopedic Hospital. This pleased some of the board members so much that they bought twenty-five copies of the paper and passed them around. All of the board members were not pleased and a special meeting was called. But in that meeting the real need for a full-time hospital chaplain was realized. So a chaplain was called and a beautiful office provided for his meeting with those with emotional and spiritual needs. One doctor said to Bill with tears in his eyes, "Philip hasn't suffered in vain."

Then back into their life came Orv "O.K." Boyington, of United Press International. Nearly every day he walked the halls with Bill and visited the children and often their parents in those little rooms all along the hall. He was so kind and understanding that Bill was drawn to him as to a brother. Orv and his wife, Janet, were a great comfort to Bill and Barbara during all those difficult days.

Because of Philip's illness, many speaking engagements came to Bill. From the front-page newspaper story, *Progress*, the Stonecroft magazine, and the *Christian Reader*, published by Tyndale House, also spread his story. One day a call came from a man living many miles away. He said, "I know you people are in sorrow, but I'm in sorrow too. I think you people might help me to find God." So he came and poured out his own story and then he too found the Lord, and knowing Him, found comfort. For many Sundays this man drove long distances to attend services in Machias.

13

At Machias Community Church, the people were being drawn together as never before. Persons who had not liked each other became friends as they shared the trouble which had come to their pastor's family. Tough men's hearts were melting and rebellious teen-agers looked beyond themselves, offering their love and help. Whole directions were changing. It seemed a little child was leading them. Miracles of reconciliation were taking place. Everywhere Bill went to speak, souls were saved because his broken spirit was proclaiming the Lord Jesus Christ. Material ambitions were dying and in their place the Lord Jesus was implanting His will. Barbara and Bill discovered that there really is "a balm in Gilead" (Jeremiah 8:22).

Then Philip became an outpatient. His little cheeks began to get rosy again and a tumor disappeared from his liver. The doctors seemed elated and his parents were overjoyed and thankful. Philip ran again and played with other children; he regained his lost weight. His happy parents hoped beyond hope. They continued in prayer and thanked God. No doctor said he was well, but only that he was doing beautifully. Another front-page story

appeared telling of Philip's apparent recovery. They took
a trip to Texas.

While in Texas, Philip began to limp. Bill asked Barbara,
"Did he hurt his knee?"

"No, dear, I don't recall him hurting his knee."

Sometimes Bill was a bit harsh and would say, "Philip,
pick up your feet." Deep in his heart he didn't want to
admit, even to himself, what he was fearing.

Upon returning to Machias, they took Philip to his doctor at the hospital. He examined the child carefully. As
evening fell, that September evening of 1967, he said to
Bill and Barbara, "We know your son looks well, but the
truth is, the cancer has spread throughout his body. There
is nothing more we can do."

Somehow, Bill's heart was flooded with great peace. He
almost rejoiced as he prayed, "Oh, dear God, there is
nothing more they can do. Now You are going to show us
what You are going to do!" He believed that God was
going to heal their son. Thousands of people were praying. Letters were arriving from all over the world, ex-
pressing concern and love, saying, "We are praying for
Philip." Money came from people who realized that the
bills were enormous.

As they drove home to Machias that night, Philip said,
"I think the worst is over. I never want to go back to the
Children's Orthopedic."

Their hearts were gripped in the midst of the experience, Bill's with hope, Barbara's with dread. He realized
from time to time with a sense of shock that she was more
realistic than he. She could recognize some of the sensi-

tive signs he dared not face.

Bill had speaking engagements that week. One was at a banquet in an attractive Tacoma restaurant. When he was finished speaking, everyone stood with bowed heads while one of the group led in prayer for Philip.

On Sunday, Philip seemed happy—almost well—as he ran down the church aisle to his Sunday-school class. That afternoon, the whole Roberts family went to dinner in the home of Al and Doris Gillet. The Winston Johnsons were there and it was a happy time. Philip fed the ducks and went for a boat ride. Winston was busy with his camera. They were all pleased at Philip's energy and freedom from pain. They returned to Machias early and Bill preached that evening, thankful for the day that the Lord had given them.

On Monday morning, Philip said, "Mommy, I'm so tired. I don't feel like getting up." It was a downward turning point as he grew weaker. Bill believed that God was going to lift Philip up: all that the skill of man could do had been done and now was the time for the power of Almighty God to work. Bill fasted, yet felt no hunger and was very alert. He was in a constant state of prayer and sensed the nearness of the Lord. Whenever he became aware of Philip having pain, he fell to his knees and pleaded for his little son.

Barbara, aware of the physical realities, nursed Philip day and night; it seemed she never slept. On Thursday her mother arrived to give her special help and comfort.

As Philip grew weaker, Bill remembered a few weeks earlier how Philip ran into the room where he was studying. He folded his little arms and said, with great author-ity, "You know what, Daddy? They're not going to have any suppositories in heaven." For about twenty minutes, he talked on about heaven. "Daddy, you know how Jesus wants to save us, but Satan wants to put us in a pit. I love Jesus." He finished his visit and was about to leave the room when he turned and said, "Daddy, soon I'm going to go to heaven."

A day or two later he was having a bad spell and Bill went in to pray with him, which he loved. Bill had prayed with him every day of his life. But when Bill said, "Let's pray, Philip, that Jesus will make you feel better today," Philip said, "Daddy, don't pray about that. Please don't pray about that!" And he hid his face. At the time, Bill couldn't understand that his little son was eager to go to his favorite place and he didn't want to be detained—not even by the prayers of his daddy.

Philip loved sunsets and in that week of September, the Lord gave him beautiful sunny days and sunsets that were gold and crimson and tinged with glory. One day they went for a little ride about the countryside to see the sunset. Philip's only words were "There's no sickness in heaven."

The next day, two close friends, Ken and Letha Dodson, called and asked, "Would it help if we just came and sat with you?"

They came, and it was a nearly perfect autumn day. Toward evening, they sat on the porch steps with Bar-bara, who held Philip gently in her arms. The phone kept ringing and Bill would answer it patiently, thanking those who called and asking them to pray. As the horizon rose toward the sun, Philip watched intently. Those great old trees fragmented the colors in the sky like the stained-glass window of a great cathedral. Between the porch steps and the church was Philip's playhouse, which his mother had recently painted yellow. It had a large window through which those sitting on the porch could see the reds and gold of the sunset. They were talking quietly with longer periods of silence. Philip broke out of a silence with one of his thoughtful statements.

"I'm going to heaven and there's a room for me there. And it has a big window so I can look out at the sunset."

Barbara, still holding him, bent down and kissed him gently, but said nothing. There was another long silence until Philip said in a quiet but amused tone, "It's funny. I'm bigger than David now, but when I see David in heaven, he'll be bigger than me."

Orv Boyington also came that day to comfort Bill and Barbara. Bill said, "Orv, he's going to be well; he's weak, but he's going to be well. It's just that I have real peace that God's going to make him well." Orv prayed with them before he left. They felt the prayers of friends everywhere about, holding them up.

Then Sunday came again, Sunday, September 24, 1967. In six more days, Philip would be four years old. While Bill was dressing for church services, Barbara's mother helped little David with his clothes and Stephen had dressed himself. Barbara was near, holding Philip in her arms. He was wide-awake, though very weak.

Stephen rushed into the room and said, "Hey, Mommy,

my friend Freddie Behling says Philip's going to die."

Barbara smiled her gentle smile at her eldest son and said, "Stephen, Philip is not going to die, because Jesus said, 'I am the resurrection, and the life: he that believeth in me, though he were dead, yet shall he live. And whosoever liveth and believeth in me shall never die. Believest thou this?' " (John 11:25, 26).

Philip began to laugh. He said, "Stephen, I'm not going to Sunday school with you and they're going to wonder where I am." Philip knew.

Stephen and David ran out the door and Bill was following when Barbara called out and he stopped. Philip had begun to hemorrhage. Bill said hurriedly, "I'm going to the church next door—tell the people to pray—be right back."

Next door, adults and children were assembling for opening exercises of the Sunday school. Bill walked to the front of the church and said, "Dear people, Philip has started to hemorrhage. Would all of you pray?" Then he ran back to the house. The bleeding had stopped and even at this stage, Bill actually thought that Philip would live.

As a mother, Barbara saw a dying child and a husband who insisted, "He's *not* going to die!" She knew what he meant: Oh, God, don't take our little Philip; don't let him die—I can't accept that as the truth—that it's really happening—happening now! She kept these things in her heart, knowing his need to protest.

Bill went to his Sunday-school class to say a few words. The door opened suddenly and Barbara's mother said, "Oh, Bill, come quickly! Philip is calling for you."

They ran back. Hemorrhaging had begun again—violently; the blood was pouring from Philip's mouth and nose. Bill called the doctor. It was Sunday and they couldn't reach him, but left an urgent message.

The frightful hemorrhaging continued. They could not hold him on the bed, so Barbara and Bill held him in the middle of the room, facing each other with their arms outstretched and little Philip between. As the blood gushed, the child threw himself hard against his father's chest, then rolled around between their outstretched arms and struck his mother in the chest, calling to them, "Mommy, help me! Daddy, Daddy!" And they could not help him.

Bill looked up into heaven and cried out, "God, God, let me die in his place!" He would have given anything for his son. Philip was worth more than the whole world. Long afterward, he remembered that moment and understood a little more clearly the words of Jesus on the cross when He died for our sins.

Down in Machias they felt for a little while that God had forsaken them—that He did not hear their cries for help. But God did hear. The hemorrhaging subsided for a time and Philip was still conscious. Bill had not known that there could be so much blood in a little boy. Barbara's clothes and his were soaked with it. Towel after towel had been soaked up. Finally it quieted down.

Then the phone rang. It was Orv Boyington. Bill said, "Orv, Orv, Philip is hemorrhaging hideously. Pray, oh, do pray! He's dying unless God does something. Pray 'til I call you back." His wife, Janet, said that Orv fell on his knees by the bed and did not move from that floor or cease from praying until Bill called him back.

Bill went down to the little playhouse that Barbara had painted for Philip that week. He sat in the chair there and prayed to the Lord. Then he returned to the house. June Thorne, one of their dearest friends, had arrived to be with them.

Facing her, feeling a violence he had never experienced before rushing out from the pit of his being, Bill shouted hoarsely, "I want to tell you today, if my son is dying, that's not the only thing that's dying. My ministry is dying. This is the last day of my ministry. Thousands of people have prayed for my son. How can I tell people about a God that answers prayer when He's not answering thousands of prayers? I can't! Never, never, never!"

He walked that floor in tears and in anger. His black mood only lasted about thirty minutes, but it lasted long enough to remember forever.

All this time, Barbara was holding Philip in her arms as he lay quiet. Then Philip began to hemorrhage again and Barbara screamed, "Oh, God, save our son! Save our son, dear Lord! Can't you hear us?"

Then Philip lapsed into a coma. Gently, they lay him down on the sofa in the living room. Barbara had heard from a doctor in the hospital that the last of the senses to leave a person is hearing. She had heard that people in comas could hear what was said to them though they were unable to respond. She had promised Philip never to leave him. Even through the horrible bone marrow tests, Barbara had always stayed at his side. Now she began to talk to their little son.

She said, "Philip, the angels are coming for you, honey. Mommy's here, Daddy's here and we won't leave you. Just rest; just rest. You'll soon be with Jesus. You'll have that room with the big window so you can see the sunset." She talked constantly, sweetly, quietly—like the voice of an angel to a little child who was about to go into the presence of the living God.

Bill slipped away again and went back to the little playhouse. Violence and anger had left him; he was not mad at God anymore. He said, "Oh, God—my dear Lord and Master, it seems you're taking my son. Then, oh Lord, I give him to You. And I'm going to love You forever, and I'm going to serve You forever—all the rest of my life and in eternity. I love you, God."

At that moment, June Thorne came and said, "Bill, come quickly."

He went back into the house. Barbara was still talking to Philip and Dr. Nelson had arrived from Seattle. The doctor told them that Philip could linger in a coma for days, or he could go quickly.

Bill said, "Would all of you pray that if God's not going to let him get well, please take him quickly to be with Jesus."

Soon, while Barbara was still talking, the little hands fell by his side.

In just a few moments, sunshine flooded through those windows and the big branches of the maple trees where Philip had played and they knew that he was with Jesus, and he was well and they would see him again. And words that little boy had said to them would thrill them forever.

When they talked about their favorite places, such as California, Texas and Ohio, he had said, "Do you know where my favorite place is? It's heaven."

Within an hour of Philip's death, a man came to the house who had loved Philip, but who did not love God. He trembled and wept and said to Bill angrily, "Now I want you to tell me about the love of God!"

Bill said simply, "I can talk about the love of God now as never before in all my life. Philip bled to death this afternoon in our arms. For a father and mother, that's agony—to watch your own son die. But, you know, God the Father loved you and me so much that He was willing to let His only Son die. And God the Son willingly took our place. That's love! He took our place to bear our filthy sins and to conquer death."

They were both quiet for a bit. Then Bill asked the man, "What if Philip had died for you and then you turned to me and said, 'I'm not interested in Philip's death. In fact, I don't think Philip was your son!' "

His eyes got big and he said, "I understand now—I understand."

"Well, you know, for many years you've been indifferent to God. You've said more than once to me, 'I don't believe Jesus is the Son of God,' when God the Father said, 'This is my beloved Son in whom I am well pleased.' "

After Philip's death, Bill and Barbara found themselves comforting others. The whole community of Machias had loved Philip since the day of his birth. Orv Boyington's wife, Janet, came to comfort them and a radiant Barbara opened the door and said that now she knew that Christ lived in her life in a very vital way, bringing comfort such as earth's dearest friend never could.

Walter Precht of the funeral home soon came to take the little body. He saw the obvious violence that they had gone through and was shaken deeply. He said, "Well, we can arrange the preliminaries of the funeral later."

Bill said, "Oh, no. We know now everything we need to know." They weren't crying now; they were at peace. Bill said, "Dr. Bob Brown will be our minister. We know the poems we want to use and the music, 'My Desire to Be Like Jesus,' and 'I Don't Care About Tomorrow.' "

Mr. Precht was so kind—he didn't come in a hearse, dressed in a formal black suit. He came in his family car, dressed casually. He wrapped up Philip's little body tenderly, as if he were taking him out into the cold, and carried him to the car.

They saw the hand of God in so many things about Philip. They had never seen the cemetery man before, yet he would not charge one cent for the cemetery lot. He knocked off so much from the price of the stone that he almost gave that, too. On it were to be Philip's name and the dates and at the bottom, the name of his favorite chorus, "My Desire to Be Like Jesus." He said, "You've given enough—and by the way, I heard you speak once." When the bill came from the funeral home it said, "Paid in full." They hadn't paid a cent. They'd sent a large check to the Orthopedic Hospital and the hospital sent it back. Philip had been conceived during a time of trouble, then born while they struggled in their first church. Dr. Burgoyne had charged nothing for his birth and nothing for his services during this last illness. The thought came to them, Our little Philip was a gift of God. He had given and given and given: love, blessings and deep instruction from a little child. Philip was a free gift from God.

The day of the funeral came. Bill and Barbara were weary from the last ten months. They had entered into God's peace, but they didn't look forward to the funeral. The place was packed. Chairs were placed in the aisles, in the hall outside and people stood.

Bob Brown talked to Bill before the service and Bill said to him, "Philip is so significant—even the way he died. I really haven't the strength or courage, but if God gives it to me, please be aware that I may say a few words."

It was a beautiful service. Then, as Dr. Brown was ending his message, Bill felt strength come. He opened the curtains, walked out and stood by the casket of his little boy. Bill was able to share the little things that Philip had said, how he faced death and how he died. Then he told them how the Son of God had died. Because He loved us, God's only Son had shed His blood for us.

After the funeral they came home to the usual flowers and food. Their little boys, Stephen and David, had been taken into the home of a kindly deacon during those last few days. When Stephen ran into the yard, they told him that his brother Philip had gone to be with Jesus. When he came into the house and saw all the people and flowers and food, he asked, "What's this?"

The thought came to Bill and he said, "It's a celebration, Stephen: Philip's going to be with Jesus."

September 30 came a couple of days later, the fourth anniversary of Philip's birth. The two brothers talked about what a birthday party Philip must be having in heaven. Stephen said, "It has to be a big cake to feed all those people in heaven. The candles on the cake must be as big as telephone poles!"

14

On the weekend following Philip's funeral, Bill was scheduled to speak five times. His first reaction was: I can't do it; I simply cannot do it. He talked with Barbara about it. Their hearts ached as they looked at their two boys, Stephen and David. The perfect stairsteps were incomplete now, with a gap in the middle which hurt cruelly. But the Lord had been so good to them; He had been their greatest comfort and they must be faithful to Him. So it was decided that Bill should go anyway. He told Barbara, "I think God is going to make it easier this weekend."

He didn't. It was very hard. Bill flew east of the Cascade Mountains to speak at a conference and the first meeting was especially difficult. The audience just stared at him with no visible response. He spent the night in a men's dormitory, filled with farmers who snored. He lay there wide-awake, oversensitive to their indifference to his sorrow. He told himself that few, if any, of them, could know about his wounded heart. He couldn't run around, waking them up, telling them that they must suffer with him. Then morning came, and he managed to get through another day.

Only during the last meeting did he share with them that he had just come from the funeral of his little son. He mentioned that the title of Philip's favorite song had been carved upon his tombstone, "My Desire to Be Like Jesus." The pianist broke down and sobbed. Bill had not realized that she was a niece of Lillian Plankenhorn, who wrote the chorus. When Bill finished telling Philip's story, she played his favorite piece and a stir went through that crowd as the message went home. This weekend taught Bill that in spite of his personal loss, there was a normal tempo of life going on all around him and that most people who are wearing their everyday emotions will respond tenderly once their hearts are touched.

Machias Community Church continued to grow and thrive. Repairs and refurbishing continued. The exterior received a coat of fresh white paint. The heating was overhauled. The floors were refinished and red carpeting laid down the aisle. A lighted eight-foot cross hung behind the pulpit. Weyerhaeuser Company had given the church five thousand dollars worth of magnificent colonial chandeliers from one of Everett's historic buildings—now wired for electric lamps. The church was more beautiful than in Bill's early dreams of what might be done.

At the same time, it became clear that it was time to move on. This seemed paradoxical. Bill and Barbara had gone from small towns to New York. There they had become identified so completely with urban life it had seemed ridiculous to come to a community like Machias that wasn't even on most maps. Now they prayed, "Dear Lord, let us stay in Machias the rest of our lives." A few years earlier and less mature, Bill had prayed, "God, let me reach millions for you—millions!" Now he knew the ego that had sat upon the throne of that young Christian. Self and personal ambition had a good share of the apparent self-sacrifice. Now a broken Bill was willing to go or to stay, however, whenever and wherever his Lord should direct.

There were increasing numbers of requests to speak at meetings and conferences beyond the limits of Machias. On the other hand, the work at Machias was rapidly becoming self-supporting and really needed the ministry of a full-time pastor. Meanwhile, Bill spoke at the Biola Conference at The Firs in Bellingham on the same program with Major Ian Thomas and others who were well known. Al Sanders, at the time in charge of Biola's broadcasting, had been writing to Bill about considering a job on the staff of Biola College in La Mirada, near Los Angeles. Because of preoccupation with Philip's illness, Bill had not answered Al. After Philip's death, he found the letter and answered it in a rather negative way, explaining that he loved working with Village Missions and their auxiliary organizations, Christian Women's Clubs.

Al Sanders wrote back, "You can't really say no to a job you haven't really looked over." Biola flew him down to look around and discuss possibilities of joining their staff. The job they offered didn't appeal to Bill because it didn't fit in with what he believed God had called him to do: to win souls. Biola was a splendid Christian college, but Bill couldn't see himself as a money raiser. Nevertheless, he was praying about the job and considering seriously whether he should take it.

Bill spoke at a meeting in Vancouver, B. C. Mrs. Evangeline McNeill, the dynamo behind Cannon Beach Conference in Oregon, was there. Evangeline wrote to her sister, Mrs. Helen Baugh, at Stonecroft, Village Mission Headquarters, mentioning that Biola was offering Bill a job.

Mrs. Baugh wrote to Bill, "We'd like to open up the Stonecroft Ministry for you to simply travel across the whole United States telling people about Jesus Christ. You may live anywhere you choose."

Bill had no desire to leave Machias, where he felt so strongly identified after five-and-a-half years. Nevertheless, with this offer on top of Biola's, it did seem that God was calling him to go on. He also knew that it was no longer right to leave the good people of Machias so often to go on these speaking trips. His congregation had been more than good to him, but they needed a man who would be totally dedicated to the work of their community.

After much discussion and prayer with Barbara, Bill wrote to Biola that he believed that he and Barbara must accept the offer of Stonecroft Associated Ministries to act as their national representatives. This would give them the opportunity of presenting Christ to thousands of people all over the nation through the Christian Business and Professional Women's Councils, Christian Women's Clubs and Business and Professional Couples' Clubs, which supported the work of Village Missions.

The sadness of leaving Machias came upon them. During the last week that they were there, the white colonial pews came, completing the planned refurnishing. Bill felt thankful that the Lord had allowed him one Sunday there after the restoration had been completed.

Then a letter came from Mrs. Baugh at Stonecroft. She wrote, "You may live anywhere you choose, but somehow I feel led that you should live near the Bay area."

They found a little home on Lester Lane in Los Gatos and Bill went on the road. Some months were fairly easy, but during many long trips he spoke every day, spending each night in a different city. He spoke at conferences, banquets, and luncheon meetings as well as at church services. Almost every day he was driving or flying to the next place—and being separated from Barbara and their boys. It was hard on all of them. Bill realized this fully, yet so many people were coming to know the Lord and to go on with Him as a direct result of this new ministry that it truly did seem that this was God's will for his life—at least for the present.

Bill spoke to the student body at Biola College. Once again he was approached by Al Sanders, who said, "Bill, we still feel that you are God's man for this job. Please pray about it."

Biola's president, Dr. S. H. Sutherland, said, "We'll give you ten days to make a decision. I must tell you we feel that you are God's man for Biola."

By the next morning, Bill was certain that this was God's answer.

Arriving at Biola, Bill discovered that they had just lost their drama coach and that in addition to his public-relations job, he would be teaching a drama course, working with the traveling drama team and taking them to the Orient.

Bill and Barbara moved from Los Gatos to La Mirada. Bill would retain his warm relationship with the Stonecroft Ministries but for now his energies were centered on casting and rehearsals with a great group of young college students. The college had taken a play to Southeast Asia during two previous years and had given numerous performances in the continental U.S.A. It was an uncomplicated play with a straightforward message and had been the means of bringing many to know Christ.

Bill and Barbara, with their two boys, would go with the team to Tokyo, then go to the Philippines where Bill would fill speaking engagements until the drama team rejoined them there.

So the pieces all fit together. After Tokyo, Bill and his family flew to Manila. Bill was booked to speak sixty-five times during fifty-five days in the Philippines—in the top universities where some of the students had been rioting, in schools of various sorts including a large school for Chinese students, on prime-time television, on the Far Eastern Broadcasting radio station, in churches and in clubs.

The drama team joined them in Manila. After doing a few performances, they flew back to the World's Fair in Osaka, Japan, then on to Hawaii.

Shortly after they returned home from this tour, a neurosurgeon told Barbara and Bill that he feared their son Stephen had cancer. There were two weeks of tests and during those days and nights they got a sample of the feelings they would have if they had to give up another son. They told the Lord they didn't have strength for another such trial, but if He were asking, they'd given all of themselves to Him. After two weeks of waiting, with an anticipation of grief they had hardly known with Philip, the reports came back negative. Stephen was a healthy boy and how they praised God!

The detailed part of Bill's work at Biola was taken over by another man. God was opening up more and more doors for Bill to do what he believed God had called him for: to go out on the highways and byways telling people about Jesus. The authorities at Biola said to him, "We feel that if Jesus Christ be lifted up, Biola's needs will be met."

Bill enjoyed his work and ministry with the students, teaching and counseling with them. It was wonderful to be used for the Lord in whatever way He willed. Nevertheless the time had come to leave his good friends at Biola and to go out and preach the Good News. Invitations to speak were coming in steadily, and he was asked to become interim pastor of The Bible Church of Buena Park, California, near Knott's Berry Farm. On February 11, 1973, Bill Roberts accepted a unanimous call and was installed as their full-time pastor.

Forgotten were those little stories he had told as a child in his grandma's chicken house in Waxahachie, Texas. He could look back with fond amusement to some of the dreams he had dreamed. The Lord had given him Barbara, Stephen, Philip and David, and had seen fit in His infinite wisdom and love to take little Philip back unto Himself.

Bill had a mission in life now; the Lord would open the

doors and point out the paths. He could not doubt that truth for a single minute, now that the wonderful words of Joshua 1:9 were burnt into his heart, "Have not I commanded thee? Be strong and of a good courage; be not afraid, neither be thou dismayed; for the Lord thy God is with thee wherever thou goest."